BROKE!

A COLLEGE STUDENT'S GUIDE TO GETTING BY ON LESS

KAPLAN

published by Simon & Schuster

New York   London   Toronto   Sydney

Kaplan Publishing
Published by Simon & Schuster, Inc.
1230 Avenue of the Americas
New York, NY 10020

For bulk sales to schools, colleges, and universities, please contact: Order Department, Simon & Schuster, Inc., 100 Front Street, Riverside, NJ 08075. Phone: (800) 223-2336. Fax: (800) 943-9831.

For information regarding special discounts for other bulk purchases, please contact Simon & Schuster Special Sales at 1-800-456-6798 or business@simonandschuster.com

Cover Design: Bradford Foltz
Cover Illustration: Kim Johnson
Interior Design: Lisa Stokes
Editors: Beth Grupper, Helena Santini

Manufactured in the United States of America

May 2005
10   9   8   7   6   5   4   3   2   1

Library of Congress Cataloging-in-Publication Data
ISBN: 0-7432-6607-2

ACKNOWLEDGMENTS

It's been quite a time finishing up this book. For their help in keeping me sane, I'd like to thank, first and foremost, Beth Grupper for her flexibility and advice, and also, as always, my mother, Santwana, for her constant encouragement. And to Maureen, my deepest appreciation for her ongoing support. Thanks also to the rest of my family and friends—for ideas, suggestions, and unsolicited but appreciated words of all kinds—who have helpfully all been, at one time or another, broke.

– Supurna Banerjee

The publisher would like to thank Helena Santini for her invaluable contribution to this book.

CONTENTS

So you're in college, taking classes, making friends, and experiencing just how liberating independence can be. Life is great—except for one thing. You have no money for food, textbooks, your social life . . . or anything else. Let's face it—you're broke!

If you've ever made a midnight run for Ding-Dongs, only to stretch that snack into dinner for a week, or tried to squeeze eight people into a room meant for four during spring break in Cancun, then you've lived the life of a broke college student. But we're here to tell you that there *is* a way to live comfortably on less. This book will show you how to do just that.

Packed with tips on and resources for everything from earning fast cash (legally, of course) to getting out of trouble when online shopping puts you over your credit limit, this guide provides you with everything you need to know to save your money and stretch your dollar further. Don't worry—you won't come across any of that complicated financial-speak that so many experts use. Our "experts" are college students and recent college grads who offer their stories, strategies, and advice—with the benefit of 20/20 hindsight—to make your financial experience at college as worry-free as possible.

Want to know the secret to living on less while still having the great college experience you've always dreamed about? Then turn the page and start reading!

GOING STRAIGHT TO THE SOURCE

Ma, Dad, I need some money.

JUNIOR, HUMAN BIOLOGY, HEALTH AND SOCIETY, CORNELL UNIVERSITY

What's the first thing any self-respecting college student does the first time he goes broke? Call Mom and Dad! Sure, you think they'll just hand over the money since you've already perfected the art of begging for cash, and, after all, you *are* their precious offspring. But this is the big leagues now and that means more money more often. Read on for some examples of what worked—and what didn't—for these college students.

Ask for money when you go home to visit after being away for an extended period of time. Your parents will be so excited to see you that they won't be able to say no to a money request!

JUNIOR, ECONOMICS/PRE-MEDICINE, UNIVERSITY OF KANSAS

GIVE THEM GOOD NEWS JUST BEFORE ASKING.

SOPHOMORE, BIOMEDICAL ENGINEERING/PRE-MEDICINE, UNIVERSITY OF IOWA

I always asked my dad (the softy) and **I always framed it as being a loan, not a "donation."**

GRADUATE, NUTRITION, UNIVERSITY OF TEXAS — AUSTIN

I usually mention how Judge Judy says it's the parents' responsibility to care for their kids no matter how old they are. IF YOU POP 'EM OUT, YOU PAY FOR 'EM!!!

SOPHOMORE, NURSING, UNIVERSITY OF MISSOURI — COLUMBIA

I have to wait for my parents to be in the right mood. I usually ask my mom first because her answer will be yes. And then **when I ask Dad I tell him that Mom already said yes**, so he's more likely to give me what I need.

SOPHOMORE, ANTHROPOLOGY, BRIGHAM YOUNG UNIVERSITY

It's just like the government—BE SURE YOU CAN SHOW A NEED.

SOPHOMORE, HUMAN DEVELOPMENT AND FAMILY LIFE, UNIVERSITY OF KANSAS

THE TRICK IS TO GET YOUR PARENTS TO GIVE YOU MONEY WITHOUT ASKING FOR IT. The first time they offered money I turned it down, saying that I was trying to make it on my own and learning how difficult it was. That's when the parental instinct kicked in and they offered me even more money, telling me that everyone needs a little help to get established. They felt good because they could still provide, and I felt good because I had more money. It was a win/win situation. Who says psychology is a useless degree?!

GRADUATE, PSYCHOLOGY, WASHINGTON STATE UNIVERSITY—PULLMAN

I don't ask my parents for cash because I am afraid of what they might ask me to do in return.

SENIOR, ELECTRICAL AND COMPUTER ENGINEERING, MARQUETTE UNIVERSITY

Even the toughest parents will melt if you say you're hungry. Yes, it may involve lying, but it's not like you've never lied before.

SOPHOMORE, MICROBIOLOGY, UNIVERSITY OF SOUTH FLORIDA—TAMPA

My parents never had a problem helping me with the costs of college when they saw me putting forth my best efforts. **As long as I maintained my performance, they kept sending the dough!**

JUNIOR, BUSINESS MANAGEMENT, BRIGHAM YOUNG UNIVERSITY

I SAVED MONEY IN COLLEGE BY RAIDING MY PARENTS' HOME FOR . . .

Things I could sell on eBay!!

SENIOR, FRENCH STUDIES, MILLS COLLEGE

Stamps, toiletries, office supplies, pens, pencils, paper . . .

JUNIOR, MARKETING, QUINNIPIAC UNIVERSITY

Old electronics or appliances they don't use anymore—like toaster ovens, small televisions, irons, blenders, and VCRs—instead of buying new ones. I'd also take sheet sets and towels, socks and blankets.

GRADUATE, PSYCHOLOGY, WASHINGTON STATE UNIVERSITY—PULLMAN

What's in the attic—you'll be amazed at the treasures you find.

SENIOR, PSYCHOLOGY/PRE-MEDICINE, UNIVERSITY OF NEBRASKA—LINCOLN AND UNIVERSITY OF MISSOURI—COLUMBIA

Frozen food . . . One time I traveled back with an entire suitcase full of frozen food.

GRADUATE, HOSPITALITY BUSINESS, MICHIGAN STATE UNIVERSITY

But what happens when your parents refuse to pay for the spring break vacation you're dying to take or that CD you can't live without? You have to start figuring out how you can manage your own money!

BUDGETING BASICS 2

I simply live cheap, eat cheap, and play cheap.

SENIOR, POLITICAL SCIENCE, UNIVERSITY OF WISCONSIN — MADISON

If I had money, I SPENT IT.

GRADUATE, HEALTH CARE ADMINISTRATION, STONEHILL COLLEGE

MY BUDGET: When the money ran out, I was on a diet.

GRADUATE, CRIMINAL JUSTICE/PRE-LAW, CALIFORNIA STATE UNIVERSITY — SACRAMENTO

I used a computer-based money management system for part of a semester, but when I made a graph that showed my average expenses, my alcohol consumption was around 60 percent of my income. That was so depressing that I quit budgeting and went out drinking.

SENIOR, HUMANITIES, FISK UNIVERSITY

I DID A HORRIBLE JOB OF BUDGETING. I have a great collection of music that I acquired in college—about 500 or 600 CDs. If I bought them for 10 bucks a pop, that's a lot of money I spent. And now I think, wow, I wish I had that money back, and why do I have a Barbra Streisand CD?

GRADUATE, POLITICAL SCIENCE, UNIVERSITY OF CALIFORNIA—LOS ANGELES

Looks like these students could have used some expert advice. Good thing that's exactly what you have in your hands right now. So read on, and learn how to manage your money.

It's happened to all of us. The waiter just gave you the check for a huge dinner out, or you have a full load of groceries relentlessly moving forward on that conveyor belt, but when you open your wallet, you get that sinking feeling . . . you don't have enough money. Is this bad luck or just a case of bad planning?

Figure out a budgeting system that works for you, especially when you're broke and in college. After all, you can't get by on less if you don't know how much you have or how much you're spending. This chapter will help you keep tabs on your money—so you can keep it in your wallet!

College students spend an average of $287 a month on discretionary items (spending on anything other than tuition, room/board, rent/mortgage, books/school fees).

Source: "College Students Spend $200 Billion Per Year." 360 Youth/Harris Interactive College Explorer Study. July 29, 2002. www.harrisinteractive.com

You don't have to create a budget that rivals the complexity of U.S. healthcare reform in order to get a hold on your finances. Below we've created a sample monthly budget for you to follow. You may think you already know how your money is being spent, but you might be surprised to discover that you're actually spending the bulk of your monthly budget on chocolate frosting with sprinkles when you thought it was your textbooks that were doing you in.

STEP 1: **Add up your monthly income:**

        Your job wages
        + Money from parents or other outside sources

        = Total Monthly Income

STEP 2: **Add up your monthly expenses:**

Rent/bills (phone[s], credit card[s], utilities)

+ Books and supplies (notebooks, pens, etc.)

+ Food (including that muffin you pick up on the way to class every day)

+ Entertainmet (CDs, movies, concerts, dinners out)

+ Emergencies (you'll have to gauge how much extra money you need to handle any unforseen expenses that may arise)

+ Miscellaneous (all those items that other people might not need, but you will)

= Total Monthly Expenses

Subtract your expenses from your income. If you get a negative number, then you're in trouble! Find a way to cut your expenses before you end up flat broke.

STUDENTS SAY: A How-To Guide To Budgeting

MY CHECKBOOK IS MY BUDGET. I subtract all known monthly bills from my overall amount at the beginning of the month and then I know how much I have to spend on other things.

JUNIOR, LITERATURE/WRITING, UNIVERSITY OF CALIFORNIA—SAN DIEGO

I calculate my main expenses (car payment, insurance, Internet service, bank service fee, estimate of gas) for each month and separate that amount from the rest of my money. Then I make sure to keep track of my balance.

SENIOR, INTERDISCIPLINARY STUDIES WITH TEACHER CERTIFICATION, UNIVERSITY OF TEXAS—SAN ANTONIO

I USE A "MONEY FOR A RAINY DAY" SYSTEM: I take about $20 to $40, put it in an envelope in my desk drawer, and "forget" about it. Every chance I get, I put in a little more, but no more than $100. Once I get up to $100 I know that I can spend it on some much-needed items or use it in case of an emergency.

SENIOR, PRE-MEDICINE, EL PASO COMMUNITY COLLEGE

My parents and I sat down at the beginning of the fall semester and decided how much money I need for the entire year (rent, bills, food, miscellaneous). Then we broke it up into 24 "paychecks" that get directly deposited into my account on the 1st and the 14th of every month. It's like having a job, without working. Some months the money is more than enough (when bills are lower) but some months it's really not enough, so I just have to manage really well then.

JUNIOR, GOVERNMENT/PSYCHOLOGY/SOCIOLOGY, UNIVERSITY OF TEXAS—AUSTIN

I divide my paycheck into thirds. The first section is for savings, the second is for bills, and the third is for going out and having fun. If there's money left over, I may splurge more that month or opt to save it.

SENIOR, SPANISH, RUTGERS—THE STATE UNIVERSITY OF NEW JERSEY

If you have or are considering buying a car, a computer, or health insurance, these are items that you'll need to budget for separately within your monthly expenses. We've broken each one down so you can keep track of exactly how much these items will cost.

BIG-TICKET ITEM #1: CAR

Things to think about if you want to have a car at college:

◎ **BUYING VERSUS LEASING:** Buying lets you decide how long you want to keep the car, and maintenance is voluntary. Leasing gives you coverage for repairs, but combined monthly costs are higher proportionally than the cost of buying the car.

◎ **MAINTENANCE COSTS:** Set money aside for gas, parking, oil changes, smog checks.

- **INSURANCE:** Payments to keep you covered can take a big chunk out of your budget. Know what you're paying.

- **REPAIRS:** Fender-benders and scratches from wayward doors in parking lots cost more than you might imagine. Check out your local repair shop for pricing info.

INSIDER TIP

Always ask your fellow students what to do when you have car trouble; chances are someone will have had to deal with the same thing before.

During finals one year my car broke down. I didn't live on campus and I desperately needed to attend classes. I talked to the Bursar's office at school and the representative informed me of Emergency Student Loans, which are provided directly by the university. I received the maximum $500 for my car repair, which was due back within 30 days. It really helped.

GRADUATE, COMMUNICATIONS, UNIVERSITY OF COLORADO—DENVER

When I was just expecting a smog check, I ended up having to get a whole new transmission due to failure of a "check engine" light.

JUNIOR, PSYCHOLOGY, UNIVERSITY OF CALIFORNIA—RIVERSIDE

Schools *love* to boot your car (attach a device to your wheels so you can't pull out of the parking space that you parked in illegally). My school only accepts cash to remove the boot. You're usually in a hurry to get wherever you need to go so you have to fork over $50 in cash.

JUNIOR, HISTORY, SOUTHERN METHODIST UNIVERSITY

BIG-TICKET ITEM #2: COMPUTER

Things to think about if you want to have a computer at college:

- **SHOULD YOU BUY ONE?** Consider the inconvenience of computer centers and printing costs versus the ease of buying yourself a system. On the other hand, if you buy, you have to purchase and replenish all the supplies: paper, ink cartridges, etc.

- **SHOULD YOU BUY YOUR COMPUTER FROM YOUR SCHOOL OR FROM A RETAIL OUTLET?** School computers are cheaper and easier to service at school, but you have more options when you buy direct.

- **LAPTOP OR DESKTOP?** Laptops are portable and expensive. Desktops won't go anyplace, but they are more reasonably priced than laptops and offer the same features.

@ **SHOULD YOU BUY A MAC OR PC?** Do your research online, at the library, or at your local electronics store. Once you understand the capabilities of both, you'll have a better sense of which one best suits your needs.

@ **WHAT KIND OF FEATURES DO YOU NEED?** Find out which programs your major requires and stick to the basics.

@ **DOES THE COMPUTER HAVE A GOOD WARRANTY?** What does it cover and for how long?

STUDENTS SAY: Computing Costs

My computer screen exploded while I was typing a midterm. My professor was really understanding. "Glad you didn't get shrapnel in your eye," he said. I stayed up all night retyping the paper. I had to buy lots of new computer equipment. Those expenses can kill you.

SENIOR, ENGLISH, BRIGHAM YOUNG UNIVERSITY

I was in a bind when my computer broke. Credit cards as well as The Bank of Mom & Dad helped me get through emergency expenses like this.

SENIOR, BIOLOGY, UNIVERSITY OF SAN FRANCISCO

BIG-TICKET ITEM #3: HEALTH INSURANCE

Options to consider if you're not covered by your parents' insurance:

- **COBRA HEALTH INSURANCE:** Extends your benefits for 18 months after you lose coverage from your parents' plan. It's not a cheap option, but you'll save yourself a huge bill if a medical emergency arises.

- **INDIVIDUAL HEALTH INSURANCE COVERAGE:** Provides your coverage directly from the insurance company, contingent on your health status and medical history.

- **STUDENT HEALTH INSURANCE:** Might be offered by your campus, making it easy to get care at school. Just make sure you know the policy for coverage during school vacations.

STUDENTS SAY: The Cost of Good Health

Make sure you have health insurance through your school and go to your school's infirmary for everything—even if you don't like their service, many health insurance plans require a referral from your infirmary to another doctor off-campus before they will deal with your claims.

GRADUATE, POLITICAL SCIENCE/HISTORY, FURMAN UNIVERSITY

During my first year in college, I was sick for more than four months. My monthly medication bill was more than $250. **My medical insurance only covered 80 percent of the prescriptions, so I had to take care of the rest.** (Basically I just charged everything to my credit cards and made my minimum payments every month!)

JUNIOR, HUMAN BIOLOGY, UNIVERSITY OF TORONTO

You've covered your bases with your budget, but here are some questions to consider if you still find yourself short on cash.

1 **WHERE IS MOST OF MY MONEY GOING EACH MONTH? CAN I ADJUST TO SPEND LESS IN ONE AREA?** If you're spending a lot of money on CDs, try to cut back on your collection; start borrowing CDs from other people or buy singles instead.

2 **DID I NEED TO BUY EVERYTHING I BOUGHT THIS MONTH UP FRONT? COULD I HAVE PACED MYSELF BETTER?** If you buy four bags of chips for snacks thinking they will last the entire month, chances are they won't. It's better to buy as you go.

3 **DID I GO OVER BUDGET? IF SO, HOW CAN I CUT BACK NEXT MONTH TO MAKE UP THE DIFFERENCE?** If you notice that your cell phone bill is high, try planning your calls so that you make them during your "free" minutes. (Remember, nighttime rates usually start at 9 P.M.)

STUDENTS SAY: The Common Sense Approach

Even though you know how easy and important it is to budget, you still might think it's too much work. The advice from college students below can help you think like you're on a budget, even if you don't actually sit down and write up an elaborate chart of your monthly expenses.

Do you need it? No? Then turn around and walk away . . .

JUNIOR, BUSINESS MANAGEMENT, BRIGHAM YOUNG UNIVERSITY

My only budget plan is to not buy on impulse. That can get you in trouble and leave you with things that you really could have lived without.

SOPHOMORE, BIOLOGY/PRE-MEDICINE, MESA STATE COLLEGE

FOOD FIRST, RENT SECOND, BILLS THIRD.

JUNIOR, BIOLOGY, UNIVERSITY OF SAN FRANCISCO

I try to allow myself to spend only the cash I have in my wallet. By taking out a set amount of money and saying that I won't return to an ATM, I limit my spending. I am less likely to impulse shop if I am working with finite amounts of cash as opposed to credit cards.

JUNIOR, MUSIC BUSINESS/PRE-LAW, NEW YORK UNIVERSITY

Don't rely on the paycheck coming on Friday to cover a check you wrote on Tuesday.

SENIOR, BIOLOGY, COLLEGE OF CHARLESTON

WEB RESOURCES

http://www.studentloanfunding.com/cstudent/manage.html – This website has a college budget calculator that will help you quickly figure out how much you might spend in a month.

www.about.com – You can search for sample budgets and a budget calculator on this site.

www.youngmoney.com – A list of financial calculators is included on this website.

BUDGET UNKNOWNS ③

My senior year I was bitten by a bat while partying near a lake. I needed a rabies vaccination that cost $1,400. My health insurance covered only half so I had to come up with $700 to pay the health center before graduation or they would not let me walk.

GRADUATE, SPEECH COMMUNICATIONS, KANSAS STATE UNIVERSITY

EXTRA COSTS

Now that you have a budget, you probably think all your costs are under control. Think again! Those hidden expenses—from parking tickets to lab fees—can easily add up to a few thousand dollars per year. Here's a heads-up on what some of those hidden costs are—and how to avoid them whenever possible!

@ "**Transportation and travel**: Don't forget to include the cost of holiday travel. You can cut these costs by carpooling or shopping around for special savers or student rates on airfare.

@ **Fraternity or sorority dues:** Charges vary widely, depending on the school and chapter. Budget $30 per month minimum, although $50 fees and up are likely. However, Greek life can have an upside; if you live in a house, the dues sometimes cover extras like laundry, social activities, and access to a computer lab.

Printing, copying, and computer costs: Stock up on printer paper and floppy disks at a discount store before the school year starts (on-campus supply stores often charge many times the going rate). You'll not only save money, but you'll avoid last-minute exam week supply crises. Compare copying prices at your school to nearby specialty stores like Kinko's—you might find it's worth the trip to save a few pennies."

Carmichael, Kathleen, Ph.D. "Beyond Sticker Shock—Extracurricular College Costs." 2003. www.fastweb.com

Think you've got your budget down to the penny? Guess again. Here are some common expenses that you may have forgotten to budget for:

- **Food:** Not just your meal plan, but EVERYTHING. Take into account snacks, dinners out, date night meals, vending machine munchies, and those cups of coffee between classes.

- **Medicine:** Even if you have health insurance, prescription medicines can add up, especially if you get a refill monthly or weekly. Budget for birth control, allergy medicine, and contacts.

- **School supplies:** You know that even if you start with fifty pens, they'll all be lost by the middle of the semester. Allow yourself some extra cash for emergency school supplies.

- **Subscriptions:** Do you have an Internet access account? A magazine or newspaper subscription? You might be charging these automatically to your credit card, but unless you keep track of how much you're spending, you could wind up going over your limit.

STUDENTS SAY: I Have to Pay for That?!

You can't always account for every cost that comes up, but it might be helpful to know what caught others unprepared. Here's what some students had to add:

At some colleges, IF YOU LOSE YOUR COLLEGE ID you'll have to pay to get a new one.

SENIOR, ENGLISH, PRINCETON UNIVERSITY

I had **NO IDEA** that you had to pay this exorbitant fee to have your computer connected to the Internet per semester/quarter. That caught me off guard! Plus, some sports-related classes charge an additional fee. For paying 30 grand a year, you would think they'd give you a break on something!

GRADUATE, MUSIC/HUMAN BIOLOGY, STANFORD UNIVERSITY

There were costs that arose randomly for athletic activities (uniforms, etc.).

GRADUATE, GOVERNMENT/INTERNATIONAL RELATIONS, CALIFORNIA STATE UNIVERSITY—SACRAMENTO

Piercings, so much beer, and trips to San Diego, Mexico, Tahoe. The things that make college a life experience are the regular expenses you don't expect.

GRADUATE, CRIMINAL JUSTICE/PRE-LAW, CALIFORNIA STATE UNIVERSITY—SACRAMENTO

Expect traveling costs for interviews senior year—especially if you live far from a city and have to take a bus or fly.

GRADUATE, DESIGN AND ENVIRONMENTAL ANALYSIS, CORNELL UNIVERSITY

And don't forget this list of things that you might think are covered in your tuition but really aren't:

- **Course materials/laboratory use:** You thought your tuition covered your class materials? You thought wrong. You also have to pay if you break something!
- **Card replacement for lost student IDs:** Fees to replace cards can range anywhere from $15–30.
- **Service fees for late registration or adding/dropping classes:** Try not to waver too much over what classes you want to take—it could end up costing you.
- **Dorm damage:** Even if you're not the destructive drunk on your floor, you're going to end up paying for the windows he smashes on Saturday nights.

Source: Carmichael, Kathleen, Ph.D., "Hidden College Costs." 2003. www.fastweb.com

QUICK-THINKING SOLUTIONS

You've gotten yourself into a financial jam and you need a solution—fast! See how these students got themselves out of trouble:

This year my financial aid processing was done late and I had less money to begin the year with. In addition, the university increased the cost of housing and tuition. Before my financial aid could adjust, I requested a 90-day loan from the university. That helped me manage before my aid kicked in.

SOPHOMORE, ECONOMICS, UNIVERSITY OF TEXAS—AUSTIN

If all else fails, donate yourself. I donated plasma. At my school, students could get up to $75 for plasma donation, which helped. I would also volunteer for psych experiments, which would pay for my time.

GRADUATE, COMMUNICATION AND CULTURE, INDIANA UNIVERSITY—BLOOMINGTON

Western Union and a quick cover story can get you out of an immediate bind.

JUNIOR, PSYCHOLOGY, CLEMSON UNIVERSITY

I DIDN'T WANT TO TELL MY PARENTS THAT I HAD CRASHED MY CAR. So I decided to get it fixed with my own money. That wiped out a chunk of my savings. There's always something, whether it's your appendix bursting or necessary car repairs. Something will come up. But if you have some money put aside, you'll be prepared to deal with it.

GRADUATE, EDUCATION, UNIVERSITY OF CALIFORNIA — BERKELEY

The emergency room at the hospital is ridiculous—do not go there unless you are DYING! You wait forever and ever, and then they charge you more than $500 for doctors and rooms.

JUNIOR, ENGLISH/POLITICAL SCIENCE, UNIVERSITY OF WISCONSIN—MADISON

At one point in time I needed a root canal, a crown for one of my molar teeth, a tune-up on my truck, and new tires for my truck. **I PRAYED FOR SCHOLARSHIPS AND TOOK OUT LOANS.**

SOPHOMORE, PSYCHOLOGY, LOUISIANA STATE UNIVERSITY—BATON ROUGE

Once you've made a budget for your money, you're still going to have to decide where you're going to put your financial resources for safe-keeping. The next chapter will outline your banking options so you can decide what works best for you.

BANKING 101 ④

I kept my bank account from home.... The disadvantage was that my parents, whose names were also on the account, could monitor my expenses. They would often call and say, "What did you buy for $XX?"

SOPHOMORE, HEALTH SCIENCES, MCMASTER UNIVERSITY

Okay, so you probably don't have a lot of money laying around your dorm room. But you should put the little that you do have into a bank account as soon as possible. Why? First, it's better than stuffing your mattress with dollar bills. Second, it's an easy way to keep track of your cash. Plus that money can earn interest, which means you'll be making money by doing absolutely nothing. Read on for step-by-step advice on the banking process.

STEP #1: DECIDE WHETHER TO OPEN AN ACCOUNT AT HOME OR AT SCHOOL

The most important factor when deciding where to open an account while you're in college is whether or not that bank has branches in your college town and hometown. If it does, you (and your parents) will have access to the account from both places, and you won't have to pay ATM fees for taking money out of a different bank. But if you can't find a bank that has branches in both locations, use the lists on the next two pages to weigh your options.

BANK AT HOME

PROS:
Parents can make deposits to your account easily.

You can access your money over holidays and summer vacations.

CONS:
Without a branch near your college, you'll be hit with an ATM fee every time you withdraw cash.

Using out-of-state checks can be a hassle, especially if you're a student. Vendors are wary of people trying to pass off bum checks, and college students get a bad rap in terms of financial integrity.

BANK AT COLLEGE

PROS:

You'll have easy access to your money.

There are often student accounts at banks near colleges that don't charge fees for deposits, ATM transactions, and debit-card usage.

CONS:

Easy access means easy spending.

If you rely on money from home, your parents probably won't be able to deposit directly into your account.

Opening a new bank account is one of those scary activities one must face upon entering college. Keeping a home-based account is fine, but if the banks around your university (and I mean within walking distance) don't match any banks from home you'd be crazy to want to pay those ridiculous ATM charges!

GRADUATE, BROADCASTING & COMMUNICATIONS/SPORTS MANAGEMENT, OTTERBEIN COLLEGE

I kept my original account and opened a new account. This really helped out because my parents and I could share a joint account, where they could deposit money for my use. And at the same time, **I have the independence of managing my own checking account** that's more accessible while I'm in college.

SENIOR, BIOLOGY, UNIVERSITY OF SAN FRANCISCO

I opened a new account. I passed the bank's ATM every day on the way to class or the subway, so I never had to carry a lot of cash and didn't have to pay extra ATM fees. Those who kept accounts at home always racked up high transfer ATM fees and had to worry about their parents putting money into their accounts. As I told them, "Grow up, get your own account, and make your own money. **MOMMA AIN'T GONNA BE THERE FOREVER!**"

SENIOR, SOCIOLOGY/LATIN-AMERICAN STUDIES, HARVARD UNIVERSITY

I opened a bank account at college so I wouldn't have to pay an ATM fee. I kept my address as my home address so I won't have to change my address on the checks each year and can save money when I move.

SOPHOMORE, ECONOMICS/HISTORY, TUFTS UNIVERSITY

At first I closed my bank account at home and opened one at school. Then when I went home for the summer I closed the school account down, because there was no way I could get money out of the bank. Now I have a debit card from the bank at home that allows me to take money out of any ATM whenever or wherever I want. I can also use the card as a credit card when I go shopping.

JUNIOR, MARKETING, QUINNIPIAC UNIVERSITY

I kept my bank account from home. My bank has online banking so it wasn't too difficult to keep track of it. I have direct deposit for my paychecks. The only problem is that when I want cash in my pocket I have to pay a service fee because I can't get to my bank to take out money for free.

SOPHOMORE, LAW AND SOCIETY, HOOD COLLEGE

STEP #2: SELECT THE BANK WHERE YOU WANT TO OPEN AN ACCOUNT

You've decided whether you want to keep your bank at home or open an account at school. But if you choose to open a new account, how do you know which bank is the best one for you? Here's a list of things to look for when opening an account:

- **Low required balances.** To maintain some accounts you have to have a certain amount of money in them at all times. Find out the minimum balance for each bank you are considering.

- **Easy access to ATMs.** Don't count on yourself to be responsible about walking the extra 10 blocks to your bank's no-fee ATM if there are other ATMs close by.

- **Debit-card availability.** It's the wave of the future. Checks are out and these cards are easy to use. Make sure there's no usage fee attached to yours.

- **Direct deposit options.** This allows your paycheck to be transferred directly into your account without you having to physically deposit it. If you are earning a paycheck or if your parents will be making deposits to your account, this is a great time-saver.

- **Overdraft protection.** This is a credit line of sorts that the bank gives you (usually a couple hundred dollars) to avoid negative reporting on your credit history if you dip below your balance. Keep in mind that this is money you have to pay back with heavy interest.

- **Carbon copy checks.** If you often forget to reconcile your checkbook or write down every transaction in your register, a copy of the check you just wrote will be helpful when you're reconciling that budget.

- **Free pens when you sign up.** Come on, who doesn't want a free pen!

> **INSIDER TIP**
> Find out the fee for bouncing a check or exceeding the transaction limit on your account.

STUDENTS SAY: Banking on Empty

I opened a new account at college, but the banks really try to steal your money. They keep giving you money out of the ATM even when you don't have any in your account, and then for each additional transaction they charge you a $30 overdraft fee, so by the time you realize you're out of money, you're negative $200 or something awful like that. It seemed every time I went to deposit a check, I would only ever get half of what it was worth because my account was always negative.

JUNIOR, SOCIOLOGY, UNIVERSITY OF MINNESOTA—TWIN CITIES

My best advice for bank accounts is to find one with accessible ATMs. Those ATM charges can really add up if you aren't careful. Also, having your bank's ATM nearby is helpful if you want to make deposits.

PSYCHOLOGY/PRE-MEDICINE, UNIVERSITY OF NEBRASKA—LINCOLN

STEP #3: CHOOSE THE TYPE OF ACCOUNT YOU WANT

You've selected a bank and now you have to decide what type of account works best for your money. The two most popular types of accounts you can open are a checking account and a savings account. The list below will help you compare the two:

CHECKING VERSUS SAVINGS

- A savings account earns you higher interest than a checking account.
- A checking account can be linked to a debit/ATM card while a savings account can't.
- You can only write checks from a checking account.
- A savings account might have a limited amount of transactions per month before the bank starts charging you a fee.
- Checking accounts usually have an unlimited check-writing policy.

STUDENTS SAY: Account Adjustments

I already had a savings account but had to open a checking account to pay bills. They are linked, so I can transfer funds between them online and check my balance online.

GRADUATE, BUSINESS, UNIVERSITY OF NORTH CAROLINA—CHAPEL HILL

Overdraft protection is a bad idea for a checking account because chances are, you're going to use it— and that means **spending money you don't have**. The reason banks offer it is because it's a moneymaker for them, not because they're concerned about you bouncing a check.

GRADUATE, POLITICAL SCIENCE, UNIVERSITY OF CALIFORNIA—LOS ANGELES

STUDENTS SAY: Account Adjustments

I opened a new account . . . I forgot to write down one of those stupid starter checks . . . BAD MOVE! It happened to be the one for $300 for my books! **OUCH!**

SOPHOMORE, COLLEGE SCHOLARS, UNIVERSITY OF TENNESSEE—KNOXVILLE

CREDIT UNIONS: THE OTHER WHITE MEAT

If you haven't been able to find the perfect bank, are finding that banking is just too much of a hassle for you, or don't have a lot of interest-gaining money to spare, consider joining a credit union. Many colleges have student-run credit unions, with specially suited options for you.

What is a credit union? According to the National Credit Union Administration website, "A credit union is a nonprofit cooperative financial institution owned and run by its members." When you put your money in a credit union, you're adding it to a large pot of all the members' money, and then members decide—democratically—the rules for the union, including how much money you need to put in to have an account, withdrawal limits, and more.

Credit unions often have the best interest rates and offer financial advice to their members. They provide loans to people who would otherwise have difficulty securing credit at reasonable interest rates.

I opened a bank account at school through a school-sponsored credit union. **The greatest advantage was that it was tailored to the needs of me as a student at that particular school.** Rates were reasonable and on-campus offices made transactions easier. There was also online banking available.

GRADUATE, MUSIC/HUMAN BIOLOGY, STANFORD UNIVERSITY

I opened an account with my mom's teacher's credit union, because there were no fees and I could withdraw money from any ATM without being charged an extra fee.

GRADUATE, INTERNATIONAL RELATIONS/SPANISH, UNIVERSITY OF SOUTHERN CALIFORNIA

ONLINE BANKING FOR THE LAZY MAN

Online banking is here to stay. And it means you have no excuse not to keep track of your bank balance, your bills, or anything else bank-related. Take a look at what you can do with a simple click of the mouse.

Make payments. You can pay your bills online and even set up payments to be made automatically every month from your account. This option gets even easier as you add to your address list, storing the names and addresses of payees you've sent payments to already.

Check your balance. Not sure if you can afford that concert ticket? Hop online, log in, and see how much (or how little) you have left in your account.

View your banking activity. This is especially helpful if you are starting a budget or you're wondering how you blew through 100 bucks in a week. You can see details of all your purchases and ATM withdrawals, including the location in most cases ($5 at Starbucks, $5 at Starbucks, $5 at Starbucks . . .).

Ours is the age of convenience. In the banking world, this means cards galore instead of cash or checks. Check out the chart on the next page to see what each card does and does not offer.

NOTE: If your ATM or debit card is used without your authorization, here are the rules about what you'll be required to pay:

"Your liability under federal law for unauthorized use of your ATM or debit card depends on how quickly you report the loss. If you report an ATM or debit card missing before it's used without your permission, [the EFTA says] the card issuer cannot hold you responsible for any unauthorized transfers. If unauthorized use occurs before you report it, your liability under federal law depends on how quickly you report the loss."

"Credit, ATM and Debit Cards: What to do if They're Lost or Stolen." Federal Trade Commission.

http://www.ftc.gov/bcp/conline/pubs/credit/atmcard.htm

	CAN USE LIKE CASH	CAN GET CASH	SECURITY
ATM CARD	No	Yes. You also get a record, and it shows up on your statement. But there are daily withdrawal limits.	PIN number— don't share this with anyone.
DEBIT CARD	Yes, you can make purchases online and in stores. There's usually no fee.	Yes. It works just like an ATM card.	PIN number—you have to sign for purchases.
SMART CARD	Yes. But it's not linked to your bank account— you have to put cash "on" it.	Some smart cards work like ATM cards. FYI—these are usually offered by your college.	PIN—sometimes. If you lose your card you're out of luck.

WEB RESOURCES

www.banksite.com – Search for banks within your college area.

www.gomez.com – View rankings of top banks with Internet offerings.

www.switchboard.com – Locate area banks. The site includes maps.

SOURCE: "Finding the Right Bank." College Move: Taking Care of Essentials, Topic Discussion. www.plansforme.com

CREDIT CARD CHARGES $\quad$ 5

I am a bad example. I have six credit cards in my name.

JUNIOR, BIOLOGY, HENDRIX COLLEGE

You've heard the horror stories about college kids who have charged up huge credit card bills that they can't pay. Don't fall into the trap. Before you pull out the plastic to pay for a DVD player just ask yourself if you have the cash to back it up. If you don't, you could end up damaging your credit. Let's take a step back from the adrenaline rush of spending and examine the ins and outs of credit.

In addition to having the ability to buy things the minute you need them, credit cards offer several advantages:

- "You don't have to carry cash.
- A record of purchases is created.
- It is more convenient than writing checks.
- It helps you to establish a credit history, which is necessary for the future purchase of high-cost items (house, car, furniture, etc.)."

"College Budgeting: What Is Credit?" 2002. www.debtconsolidationinfo.org/CollegeBudgeting.html

My advice is to **use the credit card once, then put it in a bag of water and freeze it**, then get it out two months down the road and use it for gas or something you know that you can pay for, and freeze it again. This builds your credit history, but you don't have direct access to your card so you can't run up the bill.

SENIOR, SPANISH/ANTHROPOLOGY, UNIVERSITY OF SOUTH DAKOTA—VERMILLION

Good credit has helped me with everything from getting utilities turned on in a speedy fashion to getting approved for my dream apartment. It was and continues to be totally worth the effort I put into it.

JUNIOR, COMMUNICATIONS, DREXEL UNIVERSITY

I have two credit cards in my name, though my parents are primary cardholders. I always pay my bill on time and it helps to build a credit history. **Employers as well as lenders look at credit histories.**

SOPHOMORE, ECONOMICS/HISTORY, TUFTS UNIVERSITY

STUDENTS SAY: A Credit History Lesson

I suggest all college students try to get at least one card in their name to help build credit. When you graduate and need to rent an apartment or buy a car it will give you some form of credit history. Just make sure to use it responsibly.

GRADUATE, COMMUNICATION AND CULTURE, INDIANA UNIVERSITY—BLOOMINGTON

Realize that if you have a bad credit history, it will be difficult to make any major purchases—such as that dream car. It's all about good credit . . . so don't get into any debt!

JUNIOR, BIOCHEMISTRY, BELOIT COLLEGE

Always pay off your entire balance each month to insure you have a good credit rating when you graduate. Always pay on time and never leave a balance. My credit lines started out at $1,000 per card. They were up to about 10 grand total by the time I was done, and I had no problem getting an apartment in my name after graduation.

GRADUATE, HOSPITALITY BUSINESS, MICHIGAN STATE UNIVERSITY

Good credit is better than having money in the bank because you can LIVE LIKE A RICH MAN AND PAY IT OFF LIKE A POOR MAN!!!

SENIOR, ENGLISH LITERATURE, ST. EDWARD'S UNIVERSITY

There's also the flip side to credit card spending—when you start depending on credit to get by. Remember, there's no such thing as free money.

KNOW THE FACTS: The average credit-card balance for undergraduate students is $2,748.

"Tricks of the Credit Card Trade." Consumerreports.org.

Pay the entire balance of your credit cards every month. If you can't do that, mail your card to your parents to keep until you have paid it off. Trust me, it works.

JUNIOR, CHEMICAL ENGINEERING, UNIVERSITY OF NOTRE DAME

Avoid credit cards and financing things that you just don't need and/or can't pay for. If you are a college student struggling for money then that "sacrifice" will pay off in the end. Once you have a job in your field you won't have to worry too much about what you don't have, only what to do with what you don't need.

SENIOR, PRE-MEDICINE, EL PASO COMMUNITY COLLEGE

I only use one credit card regularly. I applied for the others for the first-time discounts and regular coupons offered. You should think of using a credit card the same way you think of writing a check. IF YOU DON'T HAVE THE MONEY, DON'T SPEND IT.

JUNIOR, BIOLOGY, HENDRIX COLLEGE

Don't get a credit card, because before long **SAM WALTON WILL OWN YOU AND YOUR FIRSTBORN.**

SENIOR, BIOLOGY, ERSKINE COLLEGE

Loans for graduate school are based on your credit history. A lot of undergrads mess up with consumer debt, and then find out they got into their top law school or medical school and can't pay for it.

GRADUATE, POLITICAL SCIENCE, UNIVERSITY OF CALIFORNIA—LOS ANGELES

I had three credit cards and about $40,000 in credit available to me. My advice is that unless you can pay off the bill completely or in a month or two, don't use a credit card. My best friend graduated with $15,000 in credit-card debt.

GRADUATE, CRIMINAL JUSTICE/PRE-LAW, CALIFORNIA STATE UNIVERSITY—SACRAMENTO

Credit cards can definitely end your debt-free life. **YOU NEED TO KNOW YOURSELF BEFORE YOU GET ANY TYPE OF CREDIT CARD.** Also, you want to research finance charges. They may seem a bit trivial now, but in the long run you will thank yourself for it.

SENIOR, BIOLOGY, COLLEGE OF CHARLESTON

I had two cards—a Discover Card and a MasterCard. Most college students don't understand that **the more cards you have, the worse off your credit rating is.** My cards always got paid in full and on time and because of that, I have good credit and have had no problem getting loans for furthering my education.

GRADUATE, BIOLOGY, ALMA COLLEGE

"0% APR for the first 5 months!" "FREE BALANCE TRANSFER!" "You've been approved for the PLAT-INUM GOLD WITH SILVER STRIPES card!" All the credit card offers you get when you're in college seem like they have something special to offer besides the free T-shirts and mugs you get when you sign up in person. If you're thinking there's a catch somewhere, you're probably right. The credit card jargon on the next few pages details everything you need to know to keep yourself on top of the game.

APR: The annual percentage rate "includes the interest rate and other costs such as service charges. This is what you are expected to pay back less than the full amount you charge each month . . . average finance charges are 18.9%. Most credit card offers to students [have an APR of] 19.8%."

ANNUAL FEES: This is what the credit card company charges you above and beyond what you put on the card each month, just for the privilege of having their card. Avoid cards with an annual fee, but if you can't, remember to take this charge into account when you're budgeting, or you might end up with some nasty interest charges to pay off later.

BALANCE TRANSFERS: Lots of credit card companies send offers with blank checks attached, the 'pay to the order of' line already filled out with your name. Don't get too excited. This is just a clever metaphor for transferring your balance from one account to another by filling out the amount of your balance on these 'checks.' "If the transferred amount is not paid off before the introductory rate expires, you could end up paying more in interest than if you had kept the balance on the old card. Another hidden hit is that balance transfers are treated like cash advances, for which there is a fee of 2–4 percent of the amount transferred. For example, a balance transfer of $5,000 could cost you $200."

CREDIT LINE: "When you receive a new credit card, you're usually issued a set 'credit line.' That amount is the most you can charge on your account. Under some circumstances, your card issuer may increase or decrease your credit line."

GRACE PERIOD: A grace period is the period of time in which your issuer doesn't charge you interest if you haven't paid your bill. "Be sure to read the fine print, though. Some credit card issuers give you a grace period only if your account is paid up and doesn't have a balance carried over from the previous month."

TEASER RATE: "This is the APR or annual fee credit card companies start you off with, usually a low or otherwise attractive rate to get you to sign up. The catch is that it runs out after a certain amount of time, replaced by the traditionally high rates."

"College Budgeting." 2002. www.debtconsolidationinfo.org/CollegeBudgeting.html and www.credit-land.com/glossary.php

STUDENTS SAY: Read the Fine Print

Be aware of the 0% introductory APR because it will change in six months and all of a sudden you have to pay all this interest.

SENIOR, MANAGEMENT, UNIVERSITY OF MEMPHIS

Once I got to college I signed up for one and only one credit card—not the one with the best sign-up gimmick, but the one that offered the lowest long-term APR to college students. I swore to myself to never let the company increase my credit limit, and every six months I made a practice of calling them to get my APR decreased by a percentage point. If the person you speak to isn't cooperative ALWAYS ask to speak to his supervisor.

JUNIOR, COMMUNICATIONS, DREXEL UNIVERSITY

Don't settle for a credit card that requires an annual fee. Chances are you will be able to get another card without the fee.

SOPHOMORE, HEALTH SCIENCES/PRE-MEDICINE, UNIVERSITY OF WYOMING

I recommend starting out with a card that's tailored to your needs, like one that gives you points.

GRADUATE, MANAGEMENT INFORMATION SYSTEMS, SETON HALL UNIVERSITY

Realistically, why do you need more than **A $1,000 CREDIT LINE?** That's plenty of credit to cover emergencies and some random purchases here and there. If you have more, you'll be tempted to charge things that you want, like airline tickets to Hawaii, or the Indianapolis 500, or to go skiing with your friends. You'll end up spending a lot of money that you don't have the income to pay back.

GRADUATE, POLITICAL SCIENCE, UNIVERSITY OF CALIFORNIA—LOS ANGELES

You're at the mall and your favorite clothing store offers you 10 percent off your $200 spring wardrobe purchase if you sign up for their credit card—go for it! A lot of stores will give you the first-time buy discount. Just be careful; **the key is to call afterward and cancel the card, then cut it up**. That way you get the savings without the temptation for further use.ᴊ

GRADUATE, EDUCATION, UNIVERSITY OF CALIFORNIA—BERKELEY

You open your credit card bill and review the items . . . hey, wait a minute. You would never order from Nuns'R'Us.com! But there it is, a charge for a punching-nun puppet. What's going on here? Looks like someone—with a penchant for nun novelties—has infiltrated your account.

You have become the victim of **identity theft**. Know how to protect yourself:

- Be very cautious when giving out personal information over the phone to companies that are not well-known. Identity thieves just need a name and social security number to wreak havoc on your financial life.

- When you go online to do your shopping, check your browser setting to make sure your connection is secure so no one can obtain your information. Don't ignore the little pop-up window that says "security alert." You can tell if a page is secure if the lock icon on the bottom right-hand corner of your web page is closed. If the lock is open, it's not a secure connection, and you should avoid sending your information through this page.

- Make sure you have and use passwords on all your banking cards, credit cards, and online shopping profiles. If an operator fails to verify this information at the beginning of a phone conversation, ask to speak to a supervisor. These passwords and password questions (i.e., What is your mother's maiden name?) are there to protect you.

- Tear up bank statements and bills or put them through a shredder before throwing them away. People steal papers from the trash quite often—bills that have your name, social security number, credit card number, address—and then use them to charge on your accounts or establish accounts in your name.

The worst thing that can come out of abusing a credit card is debt. Read on to find out how to get out of it, stay out of it, and live a debt-free life!

WEB RESOURCES

www.youngmoney.com – Check out the section on credit and debt.

www.nelliemae.com – This site has great credit-card tips.

www.youcandealwithit.com – Browse through the Money Management section for information on the pitfalls of credit and credit reports.

www.fastweb.com – This site has information on credit-card debt and what to look for in a credit card.

www.cardweb.com and **www.bankrate.com** – These sites list low-APR rate credit cards.

IN THE HOLE: DEBT IN COLLEGE 6

Live like a student now so that you don't go into debt and have to live like a student after college.

SENIOR, ZOOLOGY, BRIGHAM YOUNG UNIVERSITY

DEBT CONTROL: Admitting You Have a Problem

It's no secret that college students often fall prey to debt. But the reality of it is this: You can control what you spend. How do you know if you're overspending? Here are a few signs:

- **You can pay only your minimum balance each month**. You can try to persuade yourself that things aren't that bad if you're at least paying something. But remember, any money owed is debt. And that debt gets bigger as the interest on what you owe accumulates.
- **You are buying things on credit that you can't afford.** Using credit cards to buy things out of your reach may feel good for an instant, but eventually you have to deal with the consequences.
- **You're using your credit card every day**. Instead of using your card as a last resort, it's your first choice for buying everything from your daily coffee to paper towels.
- **You use one credit card to pay off another**. This is just bad news. Imagine the bills piling up—you're only digging yourself into a deeper hole.

STUDENTS SAY: Don't Spend What You Don't Have

DON'T COUNT ON FUTURE EARNINGS.

JUNIOR, NEUROSCIENCE, JOHNS HOPKINS UNIVERSITY

Just because you have checks left in your checkbook doesn't mean that you have money left in your bank account!

SOPHOMORE, BIOLOGY, UNIVERSITY OF CALIFORNIA—LOS ANGELES

Don't be afraid to say no to your friends because you don't have enough money to do something. Chances are someone else doesn't have enough money either but is just too afraid to say so.

JUNIOR, BIOLOGY, UNIVERSITY OF VERMONT

If you are unprepared to borrow, stick with a debit card.

SOPHOMORE, ECONOMICS/HISTORY, TUFTS UNIVERSITY

DEBT-FREE IS THE WAY TO BE

Feel yourself on the edge? Can't fight the urge to spend that wells up inside you every time you walk out the door? Here are some ways to avoid falling into debt:

@ Keep your credit card spending to one card.

@ Got guilty pleasures? Monitor yourself where you know you spend the most.
Set limits and stick to them.

@ Get your credit card interest lowered. Interest rates are not set in stone.

@ Right after you make a purchase with your credit card, note that amount in your checkbook just as if you had used cash or a check. That way you'll never lose track of how much you've spent.

Don't keep up with the Joneses—there's always that one friend who has a ton of money who drags everyone else into debt. Because that person can afford to spend the money, he doesn't consider that not everyone can keep up with his spending habits. It takes a lot of self-discipline to go against the flow, so if you don't think you can handle it, find somebody to hang out with who's in similar circumstances as you.

GRADUATE, POLITICAL SCIENCE, UNIVERSITY OF CALIFORNIA—LOS ANGELES

You are a student so live frugally. You can have fun without spending lots of money. If not, study more.

JUNIOR, APPLIED PHYSICS, BRIGHAM YOUNG UNIVERSITY

Don't use credit cards recklessly. It's not free money and you do have to pay it back. Is that night at the bar really worth paying for for 10 years? If you use credit responsibly now, you can afford many more luxuries later. Who wants to be paying for a spring break trip from college when they are 30?

GRADUATE, RECREATION AND LEISURE STUDIES, UNIVERSITY OF GEORGIA

Don't spend money on completely unnecessary things. **Do you really need a new wide-screen TV for your tiny dorm room?**

JUNIOR, PSYCHOLOGY, WILLAMETTE UNIVERSITY

Don't use a credit card to buy food. You'll be paying for that dinner for months after the food is eaten—and you'll have nothing to show for it.

JUNIOR, ENGLISH, UNIVERSITY OF SOUTH FLORIDA—TAMPA

Have an "I'm soooo broke" mentality when you're shopping no matter how much money you have—it'll help you decide whether or not you need something. It's OK to spend a little once in a while, but once you're in the red, you're gonna have a hard time digging yourself out. Oh, don't get arrested/fined/cited. It's expensive.

SENIOR, MATERIALS SCIENCE ENGINEERING, ARIZONA STATE UNIVERSITY

Nobody really cares what you wear, as long as you don't smell. There is no need to spend hundreds of dollars on fancy clothes and accessories—it is just a waste of money.

SOPHOMORE, MICROBIOLOGY, UNIVERSITY OF SOUTH FLORIDA—TAMPA

Debt is a necessary evil if one wants to live above the poverty level in college!! However, to minimize debt, take full advantage of all the freebies and things that come with the student fees that you are paying.

GRADUATE, PSYCHOLOGY, RUTGERS, THE STATE UNIVERSITY OF NEW JERSEY—NEW BRUNSWICK

Being able to stay out of debt takes the ability to be creative with your time and to find ways to maximize your "fun" expenditures.

GRADUATE, GOVERNMENT/INTERNATIONAL RELATIONS, CALIFORNIA STATE UNIVERSITY—SACRAMENTO

BE REALISTIC AND REALIZE THAT YOU'RE IN COLLEGE—you should be poor!

GRADUATE, SOCIOLOGY/LATIN, HARVARD UNIVERSITY

Think there's no way *you* can fall into the debt trap? Make sure to watch out for these seemingly harmless expenses:

When students go out sometimes they wind up feeling generous and treat their friends. Be careful of too many "treats."

SENIOR, PSYCHOLOGY, CLEVELAND STATE UNIVERSITY

Alcohol will decrease your judgment and increase your spending. When you go out, go out in moderation.

JUNIOR, ELECTRONIC BUSINESS TECHNOLOGY/FINANCE, STETSON UNIVERSITY

The cost of dating is expensive. Things add up quickly.

JUNIOR, MANUFACTURING ENGINEERING, BRIGHAM YOUNG UNIVERSITY

GAMBLING: HARMLESS FUN?

Even the most financially secure student can fall into debt through an increasingly popular social activity: gambling.

In a study published in the *Journal of Gambling Studies*, researchers asked 184 college gamblers what their primary motivation was for gambling—42 percent gambled primarily to make money, while another 42 percent gambled primarily for excitement, enjoyment, and social reasons. It's clear that some students see gambling as a source of income—a dangerous road to go down.

Source: "The Motivated Scholar: Gambling in College." The Wager, Vol. 7 No. 50. December 11, 2002. www.thewager.org

INSIDER TIP

If you think you have a gambling problem, take the quiz on gamblersanonymous.org. If it turns out that you do, Gamblers Anonymous can help, or go to your school counselor or psychiatrist. If these professionals are not equipped to help you, they can direct you to someone who can.

YOU CAN LEGALLY GAMBLE IN JUST ABOUT ANY STATE if you're under 21 years old. Follow the basic rules that apply for any gambler: never bring a bank card or credit card into a casino unless you want to sit around the next day wondering where all your money has gone.

GRADUATE, EDUCATION, UNIVERSITY OF CALIFORNIA — BERKELEY

DESPERATE TIMES, USEFUL MEASURES

So far we've given you advice on how to stay out of debt. But what if you're already struggling to pay off debt? Follow these steps to start digging your way out:

- **Cancel your credit cards and then cut them up.** No excuses, no second thoughts—this is a must. Unless you use the credit card for debt consolidation, it's better to eliminate anything that will make it easy for you to increase your debt. You still have to pay off the cards, but at least you won't be able to use them anymore.

- **Make a plan.** Write down all your debts, your cash flow, and your monthly expenses. Figure out how much you can put toward paying off your debt each month. Pay debts with a higher interest rate first.

⊚ Seek professional guidance on how best to set up these payments. Nonprofit credit counseling services are usually free of charge; if you enroll in a debt-consolidation program, it will show up on your credit history. (See the Web Resources section in this chapter for the names of some of these programs.)

⊚ Consider your options. You might decide to take out a low-interest loan, consider debt consolidation, or transfer your credit-card balances to one card with a lower interest rate.

⊚ Be aggressive. Take advantage of all viable options and scrimp on your other expenses to chip away at your debt. Keep at it.

Now that you're armed to stay out of debt, it's time to discover a few resources out there that can help lighten your financial load: scholarships and loans.

WEB RESOURCES

www.gamblersanonymous.org – If your recreational gambling becomes a problem, here's where you can find contact information to get some help.

www.studentloanstation.com – This site is specifically for college students. It will help you dig your way out of debt.

www.bankrate.com – The debt section of this site has everything you ever wanted to know about the ins and outs of debt.

www.nfcc.org – This is the national foundation for credit counseling—they're here to help you get out of debt without expecting anything in return!

www.dca.org – This nonprofit consumer education website will give you tips for getting out of debt.

NO FREE RIDES:
MANAGING SCHOLARSHIPS AND LOANS ⑦

The money won't come looking for you.

GRADUATE, GERMAN LITERATURE, UNIVERSITY OF WISCONSIN—MADISON

Unfortunately, some of you might have been broke before you even got to college. Luckily, there are things like scholarships and loans to help you out.

Remember that once you have a scholarship, you need to keep up with the specific requirements that it entails. Here are a few questions to keep in mind:

- Will switching majors affect my eligibility?
- Is community service required to maintain my scholarship?
- Can I take time off from school and still have my scholarship when I get back?
- If I drop a course or decide to take a lighter course load one semester, will I need to get special permission in order to keep my scholarship?
- Are any extracurricular activities or sports commitments absolutely required by my scholarship (i.e., what happens if I receive a soccer scholarship, but decide not to play my sophomore year)?

Source: Peterson, Kay, Ph.D. "Keeping Your Scholarship." www.fastweb.com

My school would take away my scholarship if I lived off-campus.

JUNIOR, CHEMISTRY/BIOLOGY, RIPON COLLEGE

When I decided to study abroad I had to brainstorm some creative ways to fund it! I used every search engine imaginable to find scholarships. A good tip is to look for money for foreign students offered by the country you are studying in.

SENIOR, ENVIRONMENTAL SCIENCE, OHIO STATE UNIVERSITY

I applied for scholarships even when I thought I didn't stand a chance of getting them. And I did get two, so that was worth my time.

SOPHOMORE, CLASSICAL CIVILIZATIONS, UNIVERSITY OF CALIFORNIA—DAVIS

College students should be aware of those obscure, hidden scholarships that are offered by the universities for "high school seniors." They will not tell you about them during the recruiting process (i.e., high school visits, campus tours, etc.). They basically leave it up to the incoming freshman to discover them.

JUNIOR, NUCLEAR MEDICINE/CHEMISTRY, UNIVERSITY OF THE INCARNATE WORD

NOTE: Late to the scholarship game? Check out these websites for scholarships you can still apply to:

www.fastweb.com
www.colleges.com

Maybe you didn't get a scholarship, so you opted for a loan. The same rules apply—make sure you know all your loan requirements. Smart loan management starts, of course, while you're in college.

◎ First consider whether you have a subsidized loan (the government pays the interest while you're in college) or an unsubsidized loan (you pay all interest accrued). To receive a federally subsidized loan, you would have already submitted the Free Application for Federal Student Aid (FAFSA).

◎ Be aware of the requirements and stipulations for your loans (i.e., repayment dates and income requirements) and make sure you reapply each year or semester as necessary. Staying on top of the details will save you money and hassle in the long run; otherwise you could end up with less money than you counted on.

◎ Keep records of your student loans and file away all the paperwork.

◎ If your loans are unsubsidized, start paying off the interest while you are still in college. Work during the summers and school year if possible, so that the interest does not accumulate and become unmanageable.

◎ Have a payment plan for when you graduate. Calculate what you can pay off during school, and take it from there.

Late to the loan game? These are the kinds of student loans you are still eligible for:

STAFFORD: All students, regardless of need, are eligible for the unsubsidized Stafford Loan at any point throughout their college career. To receive a subsidized Stafford loan, you must be able to demonstrate financial need.

PERKINS: "Awarded to undergraduate and graduate students with exceptional financial need. This is a campus-based loan program, with the school acting as the lender, using a limited pool of funds provided by the federal government."

www.finaid.org

STUDENTS SAY: Read the Fine Print

It is very important to make sure that when you are taking out a loan, you **choose the box that says subsidized loan.** Do not choose the unsubsidized loan. The unsubsidized loan means you pay the interest on the loan, as opposed to the subsidized loan, for which the government will pay the interest.

JUNIOR, WOMEN'S STUDIES, STATE UNIVERSITY OF NEW YORK—PURCHASE

I find that many of my friends accumulated debt without knowing it by accepting the student loans that are offered to them at the beginning of every semester. I wouldn't accept a loan because I would have to pay it back after I graduate. Only take the grants and student work-study, and pay off the rest yourself. That way, you will graduate from college debt-free.

JUNIOR, CHEMISTRY, GEORGE MASON UNIVERSITY

Be aware of overindulging in school loans. I see lots of people who use "extra" money to buy the "in" outfits, and they keep getting further and further into the loan trap. What they may not think about is the fact that if they want to go to grad or med school, those loan debts will keep getting deeper and deeper.

SENIOR, BIOLOGY, UNIVERSITY OF CALIFORNIA—RIVERSIDE

Don't take out massive student loans like I had to. The school I go to is really expensive. I love it so much so I refuse to transfer to a cheaper school, but I would be better off financially if I did.

JUNIOR, VETERINARY TECHNOLOGY, QUINNIPIAC UNIVERSITY

If you have a choice between accepting more student loans to help out with expenses and credit cards—by all means choose the student loan!! It's a much lower interest rate!!

GRADUATE, POLITICAL SCIENCE, FURMAN UNIVERSITY

STUDENTS SAY: It Has to Happen Sometime

STUDENT LOANS ARE NOT FREE MONEY . . . you have to pay them back!

SOPHOMORE, MICROBIOLOGY/IMMUNOLOGY, MCGILL UNIVERSITY

I'm paying off my student loans now and have just completed a loan consolidation, taking advantage of the reduced interest rates. As for spending cash while I was in school, I had work-study positions that kept drinking money in my pocket.

GRADUATE, ENGLISH/ENVIRONMENTAL STUDIES, ALFRED UNIVERSITY

When receiving loans, only ask for as much as you know you will need. A large student loan is nice, but you must remember you will have to pay it all back when you graduate. Also, start paying off your loans ASAP, even if it is during your college years (i.e., take some of your Christmas or birthday money and put it toward your student loans). In the end, it truly does pay off.

GRADUATE, BIOLOGY, UNIVERSITY OF NORTH CAROLINA—CHAPEL HILL

As a debt-owing college student, I am honestly not opposed to debt. You go into debt to buy a house, so what is wrong with investing in an education? Particularly with subsidized loans—you can't lose. When you can get loans, pay them back after you graduate, when you are working a job that you really want and enjoy and it pays what you are worth.

SENIOR, BIOCHEMISTRY, UNIVERSITY OF TENNESSEE—KNOXVILLE AND UNIVERSITY OF TEXAS

Good thing you're starting to save money because you've got some very serious shopping coming your way—as many textbooks and supplies as your budget can handle. Make sure you survive this blow to your finances—read on for tips and advice on buying school supplies.

WEB RESOURCES

www.finaid.org – Offers information on loan consolidation.

www.collegeboard.com – Details the different loans available to you.

www.studentloanfunding.com – Includes descriptions of different repayment plans.

www.nelliemae.com – Overview of different loan types, as well as the "life cycle" of different loans.

www.youcandealwithit.com – Includes a student loan repayment calculator.

www.students.gov – Includes links to many other websites with relevant debt information.

www.fafsa.ed.gov – All the details on obtaining a federal loan.

SAVVY SHOPPING:
TEXTBOOKS AND SUPPLIES

8

Tip for getting school supplies: Check the library. It sounds weird, but you'll never have to buy another pen or pencil. Ever. Tip for getting textbooks: Always buy used. I would actually look for the oldest copy since it would have the most notes. At best they're informative. At worst, entertaining.

GRADUATE, HISTORY, SANTA CLARA UNIVERSITY

Remember when you were a kid and back-to-school shopping was the only good thing about the end of the summer? New clothes, a new Trapper Keeper, a new lunchbox . . . of course, the only thing you had to save money for then was the gumball machines at the supermarket. It seems like a bum deal—not only do you have to pay tuition in college, but once you get there you need to buy books and school supplies that can add hundreds of dollars to your bill. What's a college student to do? Comparison shopping's the way to go: If someone's got it cheap, someone else has it cheaper.

ONLINE VERSUS CAMPUS BOOKSTORE PRICES

Once you step into your school's bookstore, you're in the land of unreasonable markups. You might find yourself thinking that there has to be a cheaper alternative. You're right. Check out this comparison between the textbook prices at a leading university bookstore and at an online bookseller. You might be surprised to find that online doesn't automatically mean cheaper—but don't worry, buying *used* online saves you some serious money.

BOOK*	COLLEGE BOOKSTORE	LEADING ONLINE RETAILER
The Riverside Shakespeare, Houghton Mifflin	New: $71.96	New: $60.00 Used: from $40.21 very good condition

BOOK*	COLLEGE BOOKSTORE	LEADING ONLINE RETAILER
Macroeconomics, 3rd Edition, Blanchard, Prentice Hall	New: $124.00	New: $84.95, free shipping Used: $67.99, like-new condition
A Portrait of the Artist as a Young Man, by James Joyce, Penguin Twentieth Century Classics	New: $9.00 Used: $6.75	New: $8.95 Used: from $2.50

*Prices as of January 2005. All prices are subject to change.

TWO WORDS: eBay and Amazon. I try to stay as far away from the campus bookstores as possible—they tend to try to rip you off because they know that you have to have the books they sell. Don't be afraid to buy used, just make sure that you have the right ISBN or you might be wasting your time and money.

JUNIOR, COMMERCIAL GRAPHICS, PITTSBURGH STATE UNIVERSITY

NEVER BUY BOOKS AT THE SCHOOL'S BOOKSTORE. Go online. Why spend more, when you can buy books in the comfort of your own home?

JUNIOR, PSYCHOLOGY, UNIVERSITY OF CALIFORNIA—RIVERSIDE

You can purchase a lot of your books for cheaper than the bookstore price if you go online. Many kids across the nation are trying to sell their unwanted used books and are desperate for a sale just so they can cut their own expenses . . . take advantage of this.

JUNIOR, ELECTRONIC BUSINESS TECHNOLOGY/FINANCE, STETSON UNIVERSITY

Don't order used books online because you could end up with a book that someone has highlighted all the way through, and SOME PEOPLE HIGHLIGHT THE STUPIDEST THINGS EVER.

JUNIOR, BIOLOGY, UNIVERSITY OF VERMONT

Always buy used textbooks. The highlights and notes may seem distracting at first, but in some instances, they can actually help you study better by pointing out information that you may have missed!

GRADUATE, COMMUNICATIONS, UNIVERSITY OF COLORADO—DENVER

BOOKSTORES VERSUS ONLINE: NO CLEAR WINNER

Not everyone wants to take the cyber-leap into buying books online; plus, there are certain advantages to shopping in bookstores. Compare the following lists to see which option works best for you:

COLLEGE BOOKSTORE:

◎ Guaranteed to have the correct edition of the book you need.

◎ Used books are often available, again in the correct edition you need, but not at very big discounts.

◎ You can get all your books in one shot, with course lists available for the everyday lazy college student.

◎ Strict guidelines make it hard to return books you don't end up using after the first week or two of classes.

ONLINE:

◎ Offers great discounts.

◎ ISBN checks make it easy to ensure that you have the right edition of the book you need for class.

◎ Shipping costs can add up, especially with large hardcover books. But some sites offer cheaper shipping for the more books you buy.

◎ You can't check the book yourself to see if "some markings" means an underline here or there or the strange doodlings of a past art major throughout.

◎ You have to order in advance so you have the books when you need them.

While paying for books at the beginning of the semester is painful (to you and your wallet), there's a light at the end of the tunnel. Once the semester is over and you're finished with the book, you can sell it back! Here are three popular options for recouping part of your textbook investment:

- Bookstore buy-back policies usually offer students 50 percent of what they originally paid. Judge for yourself if that's enough for a Greek Civilization book you only cracked open twice.

- Online booksellers also buy used books, or you can match up online with people who are looking for books you have. But as always, you'll be responsible for shipping costs.

- They're young, they're looking for any break in paying for their new college life, they're freshmen. Sell to them.

STUDENTS SAY: Book Smarts

You should seriously evaluate whether or not you're going to use that Math 101 textbook, which will soon be out of date if you don't sell it back at the end of the semester—TAKE THE CASH AND RUN. (You'll never use the book again anyway!)

GRADUATE, BROADCASTING & COMMUNICATIONS/SPORTS MANAGEMENT, OTTERBEIN COLLEGE

Wait at least until after the first class before you buy the books. Many times you don't need all the books or guides the bookstore offers. The prof will set it all straight on the first day of class. Also **GO TO THE BOOKSTORE THAT HAS "GUARANTEED BUY-BACK"** so you won't lose the opportunity to get some money back at the end of the semester.

GRADUATE, HOSPITALITY BUSINESS, MICHIGAN STATE UNIVERSITY

When selling your books back to the store, get there early; sometimes they have quotas for each book and if they have met the quota for that meteorology book you're trying to sell, then you may be stuck with it.

GRADUATE, POLITICAL SCIENCE/HISTORY, FURMAN UNIVERSITY

BOOK-BUYING ALTERNATIVES

If you think creatively, you can avoid retail altogether. Some other options for getting the class materials you need:

@ **Other students**: Target people who took the class the semester before, or seniors on their way out. While you're at it see if you can get their notes and study guides.

@ **Share:** Find out who's in your classes, set up a custody schedule, and voilà: You save money and have a convenient study partner (or partners).

@ **The library:** Most professors put the class material on reserve. It might seem like a pain because of time limits and high demand, but if you're organized you can make this system work.

@ **The Greek system:** If you're in a fraternity or sorority, mine the resources of your brothers and sisters. Greek groups have a long history of passing on notes.

STUDENTS SAY: Great Minds Use the Same Books

You should meet and greet other students in your classes, especially if they have the same major as you. They can not only recommend teachers to avoid, but hook you up with materials.

GRADUATE, ENGLISH, FLORIDA INTERNATIONAL UNIVERSITY

During the last week of the current semester, stand outside a class you want to take next semester and just ask the students coming out if they want to sell for a reasonable price. The price should be slightly more than the campus bookstore buy-back amount. It helps to wave around a few $20 bills to tempt the seller. Besides, **students just finishing a final exam would love to get rid of textbooks ASAP.**

SOPHOMORE, MICROBIOLOGY, UNIVERSITY OF SOUTH FLORIDA—TAMPA

I place signs outside the class where I know my classes from last semester are and I sell the books and get more money, yet I charge the other student less than they would pay at the bookstore.

JUNIOR, TELECOMMUNICATIONS, UNIVERSITY OF GEORGIA

STUDENTS SAY: There's Always Another Way Out

I WOULD NEVER BUY ANY BOOKS THAT ARE ONLY RECOMMENDED. If they are that pertinent to the class, the professor will require them. If you feel you are missing out by not buying "recommended reading materials" check with your library, they may have stuff on reserve.

JUNIOR, LEGAL STUDIES, UNIVERSITY OF WISCONSIN—MADISON

INSIDER TIP

Don't think that photocopying the entire book is an easy way out. Copyright laws regulate how big a chunk you're allowed to copy from a book.

Check the library first for the book or ask the teacher if she has any extra books that you could use, which is also a way to get closer to the teacher.

JUNIOR, BIOLOGY, TEMPLE UNIVERSITY

Of course, it doesn't end there. Once you have the books, you need to take notes, and that means paper, pens, and other "supplies," ranging from regular old rulers to graphing calculators. Once again we checked out the prices for some standard bookstore items at a leading urban university, this time comparing them to items available at a leading retail chain.

ITEM*	COLLEGE BOOKSTORE	LEADING RETAIL CHAIN
3" x 5" index cards	$1.29	$.79 or SUPER VALUE: retail brand 500-pack, $1.67
4-pack highlighters	$3.49	$2.27

ITEM*	COLLEGE BOOKSTORE	LEADING RETAIL CHAIN
1-subject notebook	College notebook, 100 sheets, $3.25	Wirebound notebook, 100 sheets, $2.99
1" binder	$3.99	Economy, $2.09

Leading retail chains often have more specials and brand options, especially in the fall right before school starts.

*Prices as of January 2005. All prices are subject to change.

STUDENTS SAY: Demand More Supplies for Your Money

Try to save the supplies you don't use from one year to the next. Don't ever buy supplies from the university bookstores because they totally overcharge! I wouldn't pay $5 for a regular notebook that has my college's name printed on the front—I can write it myself on my $1 notebook!!!

SOPHOMORE, INTERNATIONAL STUDIES, ARIZONA STATE UNIVERSITY

Make sure to buy your school supplies before fall semester when there are back-to-school specials. Get enough for the entire year, including spring semester, because there aren't any sales then. Also, buy items such as pens and highlighters in bulk because you will run out very fast.

JUNIOR, ECONOMICS/PRE-MEDICINE, UNIVERSITY OF KANSAS

Collect all the pens, highlighters, and pencils you can from those career fairs that you attend. Trust me, they'll come in handy, and they're free!

GRADUATE, MANAGEMENT INFORMATION SYSTEMS, SETON HALL UNIVERSITY

Sometimes I use notebooks from previous classes that I didn't take a whole lot of notes in. I just tear out the pages and use what's left. I also buy refillable pencils because it's cheaper than buying new ones each quarter/year.

JUNIOR, BIOLOGY, WRIGHT STATE UNIVERSITY

I read the weekly ads for free-after-rebate school supplies and take advantage of them even if I don't need the items right now.

JUNIOR, ENGLISH LANGUAGE AND LITERATURE, UNIVERSITY OF MICHIGAN—ANN ARBOR

I use the blank side of used printer paper from recycling bins.

JUNIOR, PHYSICS/COMPUTER ENGINEERING, UNIVERSITY OF CENTRAL ARKANSAS—CONWAY AND
UNIVERSITY OF ARKANSAS—FAYETTEVILLE

ALWAYS BUY IN BULK. If you can get more for less, then why not!

JUNIOR, BIOLOGY/PRE-MEDICINE, UNIVERSITY OF MASSACHUSETTS—AMHERST

Thinking about all this money stuff can really get your appetite going. Picture your favorite food . . . if you're like most college students, you're probably salivating right now. Find out how to keep both your stomach and your wallet full in the next chapter.

WEB RESOURCES

For buying textbooks online:

www.amazon.com

www.bn.com

www.varsitybooks.com

www.efollett.com

For buying school supplies online:

www.staples.com

www.walmart.com

www.target.com

www.kmart.com

www.officedepot.com

COLLEGE GOURMET 9

Learn how to cook or get a roommate who can.

JUNIOR, COMMERCIAL GRAPHICS, PITTSBURGH STATE UNIVERSITY

You wake up and immediately think about what to eat for breakfast. You're in class already pondering what to eat for dinner. You have a late-night date with your chem notes . . . but all you can focus on is that pizza slice next to your textbook! If you're a typical college student, food is on your mind 90 percent of the time. But how do you satisfy your appetite on a collegiate budget?

First, let's all take a moment to hail the icon of college gourmet:

Ramen noodles cost about 50 cents a metric ton. You can't go wrong with ramen noodles.

SOPHOMORE, MICROBIOLOGY, UNIVERSITY OF SOUTH FLORIDA—TAMPA

The college students we talked to seem to be in agreement about the tastiest cost-effective foods and best money-saving tips for eating on a budget. You heard it here first:

RAMEN: You might think the rumors are exaggerated. But you will never see or eat as much of this cheap noodle delight in one place as you will in college.

TUNA: Tuna surprise, tuna casserole, tuna on a stick. Any way you use it, it's cheap and has a long shelf life.

PASTA: A versatile carbo-loaded meal that's filling. You get a lot of penne (or tagliatelle or rigatoni) for your buck.

FAST-FOOD MENUS: Wendy's 99-cent menu, McDonald's Dollar Menu, Taco Bell's entire menu (almost). Fast-food has found a way to get even cheaper. Dig in.

GENERIC BRANDS: Super A, Kroger Brand, Sam's Choice. You can save big bucks, especially on things like cheese and cereal. It ain't fancy, but it's food.

DINING HALL GRAB-AND-DASH: Load up on snacks for later—especially fruit and condiments. If your meal plan has a dollar limit, remember that even if you don't want to use up all the money on your lunch, you should buy as many snacks as you can and save them for later. Or if it's all you can eat, just walk in and load up your pockets!

WAREHOUSE AND BULK CLUBS: Sure it might be hard to find space for a 100-pack of mac and cheese under your bed, but these stores are the best deals out there for groceries. Plus if you buy in bulk and split the cost with your friends, the price tag gets even cheaper!

STUDENTS SAY: It Doesn't Take Much to Eat Like a King

The two big tricks are 1. Beans and rice, 2. Brew your own beer . . . an investment that always pays off in college.

JUNIOR, POLITICAL SCIENCE/ECONOMICS, UNIVERSITY OF WISCONSIN—MILWAUKEE

In the dorms peanut butter and jelly were free, so I would buy the bread for about 50 cents and live like a king on PB&J sandwiches.

JUNIOR, ACCOUNTING/FINANCE, UNIVERSITY OF WISCONSIN—MADISON

KETCHUP + WATER = TOMATO SOUP!!!

SENIOR, PRE-VETERINARY MEDICINE, UNIVERSITY OF ILLINOIS—URBANA-CHAMPAIGN

EATING IN VERSUS DINING OUT

On a night after a big exam or even just after a long day, you might be tempted to grab dinner at a local restaurant. You could even convince yourself you're getting more vitamins that way, because hey, you'd never buy vegetables for yourself. But the reality is that you save a lot of money by eating in.

For example, if you buy the ingredients to make five turkey sandwiches, one for each day of the school week (including some deli meat, a loaf of bread, mayonnaise, and a few tomatoes), you'll end up spending about $10 total. If you buy one sandwich at a restaurant, with the "house special sauce" and the fries you just can't resist because they're there for the taking, you could easily end up spending 10 bucks on one meal.

On the next page are some easy recipes recommended by college students that go easy on your wallet, don't take very long to prepare, and will make you look like a college gourmet.

- **Barbecued chicken:** Don't have a barbecue? No problem! Put two chicken breasts on a piece of tin foil. Smother with barbecue sauce. Seal up the foil and put in the oven. Set oven to 350 degrees and cook for 45 minutes.
- **Beans and rice:** Cook a can of garbanzo beans and kidney beans in a pan with some oil or butter. Boil a helping of minute rice. Combine. Stir in some salsa. Grate in some cheddar cheese. Eat either with or without tortillas. (You can add any number of items to this dish—lettuce, sautéed onions, sour cream—but these are the basic ingredients.)
- **Pizza muffins:** Spread tomato sauce and a slice of cheese on top of an English muffin. Toast or bake for a few minutes. Instant pizza!
- **Macaroni with asparagus:** Cut one bunch of asparagus into bite-sized pieces. Cook in boiling water. Drain. Cook one-half pound penne in boiling water. Drain. Combine asparagus and penne. Coat with butter and parmesan cheese. Season with salt and pepper.

- **Quesadillas:** All you need are tortillas, cheese, and a microwave. Dress them up with whatever ingredients you want.

- **Stir-fry:** The beauty of stir fry is that you can cut up any meat and/or vegetables you want to throw in. Just make sure there's some olive oil in the pan first. If you want to be fancy, buy stir-fry sauce or soy sauce to toss in at the end of the cooking. Serve over rice.

- **Frittatas:** Melt some butter in a pan. Crack 2 eggs into the pan and stir them up. As soon as the eggs start to solidify, throw in grated cheese and any cut-up vegetables you wish. Finish cooking the eggs and slide the frittata onto a plate.

- **Burgers:** Is anything easier than cooking burgers on the George Foreman grill? The secret is to season the meat with salt, pepper, and steak sauce (if you have it) before forming the hamburger.

On-campus food prices are over-inflated. I thought I was done with the lunch box when I graduated high school, but packing my own lunch saved me a lot of cash.

JUNIOR, PSYCHOLOGY/ENGLISH, LOUISIANA STATE UNIVERSITY—BATON ROUGE

Cooking for yourself is not always time effective, but if you can find someone else to help you and to share with, it makes it cheaper and more enjoyable.

JUNIOR, FINANCE/ECONOMICS, OHIO STATE UNIVERSITY

I saved money on dinner by having an apartment with a decent-sized kitchen. If my roommates and I ever didn't have enough money to scrounge together a decent meal we just invited all of our friends over and told them each to bring a course for the meal. We wound up with plenty of wacky college kitchen hijinks as well as saving a ton of money by cooking for as many as 20 people with each of us spending less than $10!

JUNIOR, COMMUNICATIONS, DREXEL UNIVERSITY

GROCERY SHOPPING ON A BUDGET

If you're going to cook for yourself, you have to be supermarket savvy in order to save money. Here are a few things to keep in mind:

○ Make a list of what you need for the week and stick to it. Otherwise you'll probably decide you need way more items than you actually do—and may duplicate things you already have!

○ Don't go to the store when you're hungry. Huge steaks and store-made cakes will find their way into your cart and you'll wind up spending more money than you need to.

○ Shop for non-perishable items like canned vegetables, rice, and crackers. If you buy too many fresh items, they'll most likely go bad before you have time to eat them.

○ Coupons, coupons, coupons. Why pay full-price when you don't have to?

○ You can save hundreds of dollars a year by comparing price-per-ounce or other unit prices on shelf labels. Stock up on those items with low per-unit costs, and comparison shop between supermarkets.

WHEN AT A SUPERMARKET, DON'T GO IN THE INNER AISLES . . . just go through the front of the store and the back, where all the sale items are . . . so much money to save.

GRADUATE, ANTHROPOLOGY/BIOLOGY, STATE UNIVERSITY OF NEW YORK—STONY BROOK

The "trick" is to get food from the grocery store and not the fast-food joint. The value of a dollar goes much further when you prepare a meal yourself (rather than purchase it prepared), not to mention that homemade meals can be much healthier than fast food.

SENIOR, LEGAL STUDIES, UNIVERSITY OF CENTRAL FLORIDA

STUDENTS SAY: Supermarket Solutions

Buy the store brand (i.e., Sam's Choice or Albertson's) instead of the name brand. You'll save a lot of money.

SENIOR, POLITICAL SCIENCE, UNIVERSITY OF OKLAHOMA

Don't carry your debit card around with you because you'll tend to spend more than is necessary. Just withdraw the cash beforehand. Then you won't spend more than you planned because you won't have access to the money.

SOPHOMORE, ANTHROPOLOGY, BRIGHAM YOUNG UNIVERSITY

Every grocery store in town had flyers in the local newspaper stating all of the great sales on food. Watching and partaking in this shopping strategy allowed anybody to eat everything their body needed as long as they had a freezer to stock up.

GRADUATE, POLITICAL SCIENCE, CENTRAL WASHINGTON UNIVERSITY

MEAL PLAN GETTING YOU DOWN?

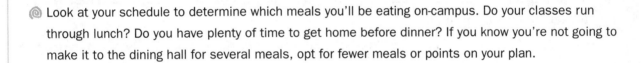

Sure it's cheap to eat in, but when grocery shopping gets you down, it's nice to have a meal plan to fall back on. Here are some money-saving tips for eating on-campus:

- Look at your schedule to determine which meals you'll be eating on-campus. Do your classes run through lunch? Do you have plenty of time to get home before dinner? If you know you're not going to make it to the dining hall for several meals, opt for fewer meals or points on your plan.

- Most colleges have two types of meal plans: one where you get a certain amount of meals per day and one where you have a balance of money per month to spend. If you're a grazer who likes to eat a little each time and make many return trips, the latter plan is probably for you. If you like to eat a lot all at once and get hungry according to a schedule, the first plan is your best bet.

When your meal plan runs out . . . **make lots of dinner dates with people who still have money on their meal plan** and get them to pay.

JUNIOR, GOVERNMENT/COMPUTER SCIENCE, WESLEYAN UNIVERSITY

We understand that sometimes you just want to eat out, and every college student deserves this luxury once in a while. But will it put your bank account in jeopardy? Not if you follow the smart dining tips on the next two pages!

◉ "Consider going for the Early Bird Specials to save some money.

◉ Use a frequent dining card. You can join discount-dining programs such as Dining à la Card, Dinner on Us, or Entertainment. Call restaurants to see if they are a member of any program and find out about the discounts they offer.

@ Share salads and desserts with your dining partner.

@ If you do not have a big appetite, share an entrée.

@ Drink water instead of other beverages.

@ Bring leftovers home."

www.youcandealwithit.com

I guess I never took into account how **EATING OUT REALLY DOES ADD UP**. At times, it's just inconvenient to go through the trouble of making food—especially when you're pressed for time—so you usually end up finding yourself scarfing down something at the nearest fast-food chain. I usually try to avoid this by making a whole lot of food on the weekend that can last me through the week.

JUNIOR, PSYCHOLOGY, UNIVERSITY OF CALIFORNIA—DAVIS

The amount of money I spent eating out on the weekends was surprising. The weekend meals on-campus were mediocre and I would eat out a lot on weekends. Money went very fast this way.

GRADUATE, BIOLOGY, UNIVERSITY OF ST. THOMAS

STUDENTS SAY: Get Creative

We usually complained about the pizza we ordered, so we would get a credit on our account for a free pizza the next time. They eventually caught on to us.

GRADUATE, HEALTH CARE ADMINISTRATION, STONEHILL COLLEGE/UNIVERSITY OF NEW ENGLAND

I worked for school events where food was provided.

SENIOR, BIOLOGY, REED COLLEGE

I USE THE COUPON BOOKLETS **that are passed out all over campus because a lot of coupons for college students involve restaurants. I also have lots of friends who work in restaurants, so I eat there and get a discount or free food.**

SOPHOMORE, BIOLOGY/PSYCHOLOGY, COLORADO STATE UNIVERSITY

I worked in bars/restaurants/coffee shops. I got to eat and drink the mistakes and the experiments. Free coffee and a free meal per shift were incentive enough—and I got paid!

GRADUATE, BIOLOGY, MOORHEAD STATE UNIVERSITY

It is always great if you have a close friend who you can eat with because that way you can BUY A FOOT-LONG SUB AND SHARE THE FOOD AND THE EXPENSE, which comes out to be much less.

SENIOR, PSYCHOLOGY, UNIVERSITY OF MIAMI—CORAL GABLES

If you visit a restaurant frequently, such as a deli, **make sure to pick up a punch card so that you can get free items after buying the designated amount of items.**

JUNIOR, ECONOMICS/PRE-MEDICINE, UNIVERSITY OF KANSAS—LAWRENCE

If you have a car, don't get delivery.

SENIOR, POLITICAL SCIENCE/INTERNATIONAL STUDIES, NORTHWESTERN UNIVERSITY

24-hour donut places are the best. Between 4–5 A.M. they throw out all the donuts from the day before.

SOPHOMORE, HUMAN DEVELOPMENT AND FAMILY LIFE, UNIVERSITY OF KANSAS

I am sad to admit that I have brought plastic baggies to local buffet-style restaurants and hoarded cookies to take home.

SENIOR, INTERPERSONAL COMMUNICATION, PURDUE UNIVERSITY

Make sure that you are friends with students who have parents in the area, so that you get invited over to their house for dinner. The benefits don't end there. **SNACKS, FREE LAUNDRY....**

SENIOR, BIOLOGY, CORNELL UNIVERSITY

I went to college in Los Angeles, and my friends and I would look for casting calls for extras, where all they do is **pay you in food.** So we'd go, take our books, study for the day, and eat for free.

GRADUATE, POLITICAL SCIENCE, UNIVERSITY OF CALIFORNIA — LOS ANGELES

Once your stomach is full, you'll probably want to relax and have fun for a while. But just like good food, a good time costs money. Read on for some expert tips from students on how to entertain yourself on a tight budget.

WEB RESOURCES

www.collegeclub.com – Register at this site for free, then visit the "Eating for Cheap" forum to read posts from other students about dining for less.

www.aboutcollege.com – You'll find a large list of recipes submitted by college students that take into account the college student's budget and cooking resources.

www.studentadvantage.com – Get a card at this site that can save you money at restaurants for those times when you just have to get some off-campus food.

Browse your school's website or campus life website for ideas for cheap eats. If you don't find anything, get the conversation started—everyone wants to talk/write/dream about food!

ENTERTAINMENT VALUE 10

The most fun things happen when you don't plan anything.

GRADUATE, CRIMINAL JUSTICE/PRE-LAW, CALIFORNIA STATE UNIVERSITY — SACRAMENTO

In between all the studying, eating, and budgeting, a college student's gotta have time for some fun. Unfortunately, fun costs money. Movies, eating out, hitting the bars—everything you want to do during your down-time comes with a tab. If you need some cheap entertainment options, look no farther than your very own campus.

- **The library:** Most college libraries have extensive collections of videos, DVDs, and CDs. Of course, they have books and magazines, too—remember when reading used to be fun?

- **Club events:** Fraternities and sororities will often have free parties, but Greek life isn't your only option. Check out parties offered by the French club or pizza nights courtesy of the College Democrats.

- **School-sponsored events:** Spring concerts, sporting events, student theater, art exhibits, dances, lectures—grab an events calendar and take advantage of these free (or discounted) options while you can.

- **Game rooms on-campus:** Pool tables, foosball, air hockey—rediscover your inner child and let off some steam, either for free or for a few bucks.

There are a lot of activities offered on-campus that are free. I have found that these are even more fun than the regular outings to the movie theater. You also meet new friends doing this kind of stuff.

JUNIOR, BIOLOGY, UNIVERSITY OF PORTLAND

We have a place in our dorm where we can check out board games, laser tag equipment, and more for free.

JUNIOR, BIOCHEMISTRY, UNIVERSITY OF WISCONSIN—MADISON

Most universities have a campus activities/recreation board that organizes all kinds of events and charges little to no money. **MY UNIVERSITY ALSO HAS LISTSERVES YOU CAN SUBSCRIBE TO** and receive emails about campus goings-on.

JUNIOR, LIBERAL STUDIES, UNIVERSITY OF SOUTH FLORIDA

HOW TO ID A DEAL

Thankfully, someone somewhere figured out that college students would always be broke. Thus, the student ID was created. Don't think your student savings are limited to movies; with your ID card you can get a break on everything from meals to photocopying costs to museum visits. And don't be afraid to ask if there's a student discount—every buck counts.

USE YOUR DISCOUNT HERE

In addition to getting discounts with your student ID, if you want to pay a small fee for a Student Advantage card you can get discounts at places such as these:

Amtrak
The New York Times Electronic Edition
Loews Cineplex
Office Depot

Foot Locker
Barnes & Noble.com
UrbanOutfitters.com

Source: www.studentadvantage.com

At many places, you can get discounts with your student ID, whether it be for a movie, concert, restaurant, travel for spring break, etc.

GRADUATE, COMMUNICATION AND CULTURE, INDIANA UNIVERSITY—BLOOMINGTON

Whenever you go out to shop for anything, **YOU SHOULD ALWAYS ASK IF THERE IS A STUDENT DISCOUNT.** Most people don't ask because they are shy, but most schools either have cards that they give out to students as a proof of membership, or students have to simply show their ID.

JUNIOR, BIOLOGY, STATE UNIVERSITY OF NEW YORK—STONY BROOK

ON-SCREEN ENTERTAINMENT

No doubt about it, TV is the main source of entertainment for the average college student. But even the most diehard couch potato goes out to rent a movie once in a while, or maybe even relocates to a movie theater for a change. Here are some ways to save money on movies, wherever you choose to watch them:

- If you rent more than five movies a month, online rental services are for you! For about 20 bucks a month, you can get movies from a list you make online. Plus they'll send the movies right to your dorm or apartment and you simply mail them back (postage paid) when you're done.

- The local video store near your college is guaranteed to rent movies at lower prices than the national chains.

- Instead of the normal $10 you'll pay to go to the movies, use your student ID to get a discounted rate—usually $3–5 off. You can also check out special movie showings on-campus, which often have a cultural or academic theme.

- When all else fails, trade movies with a friend! It's easy, it's free, and you'll get some great recommendations.

INSIDER TIP

Check out imdb.com for movie synopses, cast listings, user ratings, and other fun trivia on every movie under the sun.

STUDENTS SAY: Movie Mania

FIND A FRIEND WITH A CAMCORDER and make a movie, or watch movies. Also, be sure to know where all the free stuff is being given out.

JUNIOR, GOVERNMENT/COMPUTER SCIENCE, WESLEYAN UNIVERSITY

We would have fun for less with a group of friends by downloading movies off the Internet and camping out in front of the computer for a movie night.

SENIOR, PSYCHOLOGY, TEXAS CHRISTIAN UNIVERSITY

When the regular options just don't cut it, you're going to have to stretch your academically overloaded mind to figure out fun ways to keep yourself busy. Read on to find out what some students did when they got bored in college:

Lots and lots of creative (read "mindless") activities involving **improv acting in public places** and looking for girls!

JUNIOR, BUSINESS MANAGEMENT, BRIGHAM YOUNG UNIVERSITY

We spent time together, usually borrowing each other's beauty supplies and having a "SPA NIGHT."

GRADUATE, HEALTH CARE ADMINISTRATION, STONEHILL COLLEGE/UNIVERSITY OF NEW ENGLAND

We would rent a PlayStation with a couple of games and have tournaments.

GRADUATE, PSYCHOLOGY, WASHINGTON STATE UNIVERSITY

We worked in the bars. We drank and socialized, had fun, and got tips for it.

GRADUATE, BIOLOGY, MOORHEAD STATE UNIVERSITY

When we were all single, we would go out to the bars. There were always guys willing to buy us drinks.

JUNIOR, ACCOUNTING, UNIVERSITY OF ALABAMA—TUSCALOOSA

GO WINDOW SHOPPING!

SENIOR, ENVIRONMENTAL STUDIES, HUNTER COLLEGE

My roommates and I would go outside a lot and play Frisbee or have water gun battles or snowball fights. We got into the habit of going to Wal-Mart or Sheetz for fun too . . . especially at 3 A.M. . . . YOU'D BE AMAZED AT WHAT YOU WILL SEE AT THIS TIME OF THE MORNING.

SENIOR, PSYCHOLOGY/ELEMENTARY EDUCATION,
INDIANA UNIVERSITY OF PENNSYLVANIA AND SAINT VINCENT COLLEGE

It sounds dumb, but we played board games like Pictionary . . . of course alcohol was usually involved, so that's not totally without expense.

JUNIOR, ENGLISH, UNIVERSITY OF PUGET SOUND AND SOUTHERN METHODIST UNIVERSITY

We enjoyed camping . . . whether at a park or in my backyard!

SENIOR, BIOLOGY, UNIVERSITY OF ARKANSAS

If you live in a city, take the subway to a stop you've never been to and check it out. Use coupons and student rates to check out museums.

SOPHOMORE, ECONOMICS/HISTORY, TUFTS UNIVERSITY

The on-campus gyms allow people to bond while getting physical exercise, too.

JUNIOR, BIOLOGY/PRE-MEDICINE, UNIVERSITY OF MASSACHUSETTS—AMHERST

My friends and I talk on the phone, have gossip sessions, watch TV, and play video games. Any activity outside is also very helpful. Sitting in the middle of campus having lunch is nice.

JUNIOR, PSYCHOLOGY, UNIVERSITY OF CALIFORNIA—RIVERSIDE

My friends and I go to the beach a lot. It's pretty cheap if we all split gas prices. So is hiking, biking, and camping.

JUNIOR, PSYCHOLOGY, WILLAMETTE UNIVERSITY

Look in the school newspaper or the regular newspaper for free or low-cost events.

SENIOR, POLITICAL SCIENCE, UNIVERSITY OF NEBRASKA—OMAHA

We went to Barnes & Noble and sat on their couches and read through comic books and magazines.

JUNIOR, ART/PSYCHOLOGY, EAST CAROLINA UNIVERSITY

Watching theater majors rehearsing for plays is hilarious—just walk into the auditoriums and sit down.

SOPHOMORE, MICROBIOLOGY, UNIVERSITY OF SOUTH FLORIDA—TAMPA

ROAD TRIPS!!!! They are so much fun and really not expensive if you plan wisely. We used to hop in the car and go visit other friends at different colleges. It was so much fun and all we had to pay for were our drinks and a few meals.

SENIOR, BIOMEDICAL SCIENCE/ANTHROPOLOGY, STATE UNIVERSITY OF NEW YORK—BUFFALO

Most people spend money when they're bored. **Plan your time wisely,** and in a way, you can save yourself money by having fun.

GRADUATE, POLITICAL SCIENCE, UNIVERSITY OF CALIFORNIA—LOS ANGELES

Be aware of the entertainment specific to your region or school. For instance, did you know **you can get free massages** at a lot of schools from students in the athletic-trainer programs?

JUNIOR, ENGLISH, UNIVERSITY OF DALLAS

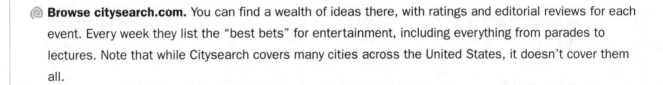

You just scored a date with your biggest crush and you want to go somewhere fantastic. The problem? "Fantastic" is just too expensive these days! Don't despair. Here are some ideas for fun, inexpensive dates:

- **Browse citysearch.com.** You can find a wealth of ideas there, with ratings and editorial reviews for each event. Every week they list the "best bets" for entertainment, including everything from parades to lectures. Note that while Citysearch covers many cities across the United States, it doesn't cover them all.

- **Check on-campus events.** Japanese mask-making could be just as romantic and a lot more fun than thinning out the contents of your wallet on an expensive meal with small, artfully-placed portions.

- **Go for a walk.** You can save money, get to know each other better, and get some exercise in, all at the same time.

- **Explore the great outdoors.** Go to the beach or the park and bring a picnic along to personalize the experience.

- **Cook dinner together.** The possibilities are endless. Make spaghetti and meatballs for two à la *Lady and the Tramp,* or split a tossed salad and garlic bread (don't forget the breath mints).

The fun doesn't stop here. You can also decide to go Greek. But is joining a fraternity or sorority a good value or an unnecessary expense?

WEB RESOURCES

www.netflix.com – For $19.95 a month, get as many DVDs as you want—three at a time. Includes user ratings, if you're wondering if you really want to get *Swamp Thing*.

www.imdb.com – Database of actors, movies, TV shows. Includes cast listings, fun trivia, and user synopses.

www.citysearch.com – If your city is covered by this site, you can find things to do on weekends and read editorial reviews on restaurants, local attractions, and other entertainment options.

THE COST OF GREEK LIFE 11

I must own more than 30 Greek T-shirts that I did not want.

SENIOR, INTERPERSONAL COMMUNICATION, PURDUE UNIVERSITY

So you want to go Greek? It can be tons of fun, but like any extracurricular activity, it's going to cost you money to join. Don't be surprised to find out that you'll start spending before you're even a full-fledged member. In fact, the first year is the most expensive. Initiation fees for pledges can cost several hundred dollars.

Check out these additional things you might be expected to dole out money for before you become a member:

- **Clothing for pledging:** They may be neon or in other ways embarrassing, but expect a uniform of sorts to make it obvious you're a pledge.

- **Group activities:** Whether it's dinner or a road trip, part of pledging means joining in when they tell you to, so be prepared for whatever cost comes along with these activities.

- **Supplies:** You might be called on to make posters for members of your frat or sorority, or design a decorative piñata for a theme party. Try to get creative with your resources so you can save money. Look around your room or even in your classrooms (no "borrowing"!) for things you can use.

We used to borrow the pledges' IDs and use their unlimited dining passes to eat for free.

GRADUATE, HOSPITALITY BUSINESS, MICHIGAN STATE UNIVERSITY

What about how much it costs to buy clothes for rush (recruitment for those of you that like to be proper)!

JUNIOR, MARKETING, ARIZONA STATE UNIVERSITY

PAYING YOUR DUES

If you join a fraternity or sorority, add dues to your monthly or yearly costs. Just like pledging fees, dues cover the cost of Greek activities and general living. Know the facts:

- According to the students surveyed for this book, the average cost of Greek life is $1,600 per year. Respondents paid anywhere from $100 to $9,000 per year to be a member of a sorority or fraternity.

- When it comes to annual fees, all Greek organizations are not the same. The difference in cost between certain sectors of Greek life can be explained by whether or not the organizations you're considering are national or local. Local chapters that are part of a large national organization are required to pay a certain amount each year to the national fund, as well as covering all their own expenses. Frats that are strictly local have to pay for only what they need for frat activities, food, and other expenses.

- Greek life is social life. In addition to your dues you will be paying for formals, materials for community service projects, and more.

- If you live outside the house, you'll not only have to pay for your own housing costs, but you'll be paying for the upkeep of the fraternity or sorority house as well.

STUDENTS SAY: Are the Annual Costs Worth It?

I have to pay **$600 a year** total for insurance, dues, and fees. However I don't physically see where any of that money goes. Anything that we do as a fraternity requires even more money, usually an extra 20 bucks a week or so.

JUNIOR, ELECTRONIC BUSINESS TECHNOLOGY/FINANCE, STETSON UNIVERSITY

I am in a sorority and I spend about **$4,000 A YEAR** on dues, including house bills and national dues.

SOPHOMORE, BIOCHEMISTRY & MOLECULAR BIOLOGY/PRE-MEDICINE, OKLAHOMA STATE UNIVERSITY

I was in a sorority for about a year and a half. I spent all of my savings on being a part of this organization. When you first enter, you spend about $600, not including monthly dues of $37. I probably spent more than $1,000 JUST FOR MEMBERSHIP.

GRADUATE, BIOLOGY, UNIVERSITY OF TEXAS—SAN ANTONIO

You work it all out and you figure you can cover the dues. Remember that any activity has hidden expenses. Below are some of the extra costs associated with Greek life, plus some tips for trimming these expenses.

◉ **Greek paraphernalia.** Whether you want to or not, you will buy many items items emblazoned with your house letters. If you already have more items than you can possibly wear, just say no!

◉ **"Sibling" costs.** Even when you take into account extra costs for yourself, remember that many fraternities and sororities have extensive activities and gift exchanges between senior members and new pledges. To save some cash, why not make a present instead of purchasing one!

Parties/Formals. This is why you joined Greek life. This is what's going to cost you the most. You have to fund these events and also rent tuxes, buy dresses, and make costumes. Exchange outfits and accessories with your brothers and sisters to keep costs down.

Charity events. All fraternies and sororities perform some sort of community service. Whether it's fundraising for the local animal shelter or cleaning up a community park, expect to spend time and money on charity. If your budget's tight, volunteer your time instead of your money.

Sharing food with a house full of people. Don't be surprised if your bulk pack of 20 bagels is missing the day after you buy it. Most of the food in the house will be provided for you—try to make do with what's available, and you'll save money. Or you could always hide extra food in your room!

⊚ **Commemorative photos.** Many colleges have a system where someone comes and takes pictures at parties and events and then you can look through the proofs and buy them. Ask yourself, "Do I really need this picture with the same people I've already taken 65 other pictures with?" before buying . . . or bring your own camera or purchase a disposable camera and capture your own memories.

⊚ **Fees for not attending an event.** The rules differ for every fraternity or sorority, but if you miss an event or fail to perform certain duties, you are often charged for your slip-up.

STUDENTS SAY: You Will Pay

The extra fees that they don't tell you about are the initiation pin, the endless T-shirts, donations for philanthropy, social events such as mixers, semi-formals, and formals, and sisterhood events.

SENIOR, PRE-LAW CRIMINOLOGY/ENGLISH LITERATURE, UNIVERSITY OF MIAMI

In sororities, **there is a semester where you are a "Big Sister" to a new pledge,** which can cost a couple hundred dollars.

JUNIOR, PSYCHOLOGY, UNIVERSITY OF VIRGINIA

I did not expect all the contributions we had to make to charity, and WE GOT FINED FOR EVERYTHING. We also had to pay for our T-shirts, our date's T-shirts, dates to our parties, pictures, etc. It got to be very expensive and annoying.

GRADUATE, BUSINESS, UNIVERSITY OF MISSISSIPPI

Each week we had to pay at least $15 for mixers or social events on- or off-campus. Plus we would buy decorations and the money would always come out of our pockets instead of the treasury.

JUNIOR, BIOLOGY, PENNSYLVANIA STATE UNIVERSITY

Costs for social events were often paid out-of-pocket. Fortunately, our organization solicited funding from our university's student government and held fund-raisers, which minimized the amount of spending required from its members.

SENIOR, LEGAL STUDIES, UNIVERSITY OF CENTRAL FLORIDA

A lot of money is spent on things you don't HAVE to buy—like T-shirts and dance favors. It's hard to resist and not buy them because you want the souvenirs. Just plan for those expenses as well.

JUNIOR, BIOLOGY, ILLINOIS WESLEYAN UNIVERSITY

NO PAIN, NO GAIN

You'll find many pledges who complain about the time and money they have to put into joining a fraternity or sorority. But in the end, you'll be hard-pressed to find many people who don't loyally stand by their Greek experience. You make friends and have fun, and you'll have networking connections for the rest of your life. Sororities have created many networking opportunities that weren't available to women a short time ago. As for fraternities, consider this:

According to forbes.com, 120 of the Forbes 200 chief executive officers were fraternity members. Seems like the old boys' network is still alive and kicking. If you're looking to become the CEO of a major company, check out the next page for a list of fraternities you might want to consider joining.

BEST FRATERNITIES FOR FUTURE CEOS

Fraternity	Members Who Are Forbes 500s CEOs
Beta Theta Pi	11
Sigma Alpha Epsilon	9
Sigma Chi	9
Lambda Chi Alpha	8
Alpha Tau Omega	7

Source: Dukcevich, Davide. "Best Fraternities for Future CEOs." January 31, 2003. forbes.com

STUDENTS SAY: It All Works Out in the End

I pay around $1,600 a year for dues in my fraternity; however, it cuts the cost of how much I have to spend for partying throughout the semester.

JUNIOR, HUMAN BIOLOGY, CORNELL UNIVERSITY

You get some great deals and it's well worth the money. My dues were $500 per semester. I easily got that back with all the events we did. Good investment.

SENIOR, MATERIALS SCIENCE ENGINEERING, ARIZONA STATE UNIVERSITY

I spent approximately $5,500 a year, which sounds like a lot but ended up being cheaper than living in an apartment, paying utilities, and buying all my own food.

GRADUATE, BIOLOGY, UNIVERSITY OF SOUTHERN CALIFORNIA

I am currently in a fraternity, and I recommend it for every incoming student. However, I am in debt a lot to my fraternity.

JUNIOR, MICRO/MOLECULAR BIOLOGY, UNIVERSITY OF CENTRAL FLORIDA

It is the most FUN I ever had in my life despite all of the expenses . . . so, if you can afford it, do it, and if you can't, there are always payment plans!!

JUNIOR, MARKETING, ARIZONA STATE UNIVERSITY

I cannot afford the $800 to get into the sorority I want to be in. I would also have to pay an additional $200 per year. That is unrealistic to me.

SENIOR, COMMUNICATION, UNIVERSITY OF PENNSYLVANIA

I was a member for about two weeks, but I was always broke due to their fees so I just decided to skip that whole experience. I'm better off now than I was then. I HAVE MORE PRIVACY AND MORE MONEY TO MY NAME AT THE END OF THE DAY.

SENIOR, PRE-MEDICINE, EL PASO COMMUNITY COLLEGE

BY THE TIME YOU'RE A SENIOR, you end up hanging out at places that don't involve your fraternity or sorority. Also, at most Greek events, the members can invite whomever they want. You don't have to be a member of that sorority or fraternity to attend the fun parties. Decide whether or not Greek life is worth the cost just for the social scene.

SENIOR, ECONOMICS, UNIVERSITY OF CALIFORNIA—SANTA CRUZ

There are tons of ways to have fun in college—it doesn't end with Greek life and going to the movies. After all, we still haven't talked about the craziest, all-out fun time of year: SPRING BREAK.

FUN IN THE SUN: SPRING BREAK 12

Spring break is an awesome time. It's the ultimate release for college students who deal with a lot of stress. I wouldn't go as far as saying it's as crazy as on MTV . . . wait, I take that back. Yes it is.

SOPHOMORE, MICRO/MOLECULAR BIOLOGY, UNIVERSITY OF CENTRAL FLORIDA

SPRING BREAK FEVER

Okay, so you don't have that much money, but you just *can't* pass up going on spring break with your friends! What's a strapped-for-cash student to do? Before we tell you about all the great deals you can find, keep in mind that some deals *are* too good to be true. A spring break scam is a sure-fire way to wind up broke. Take a look at the student experiences on the next few pages.

A few girlfriends found an "all expenses included" deal to Cancun for seven days . . . great price. It turns out that "all expenses included" includes an imaginary hotel with an imaginary pool with a fabulous imaginary swim-up bar.

SENIOR, PRE-MEDICINE, KENT STATE UNIVERSITY

A couple of my classmates were stranded in Mexico because the travel agency "forgot" to mention that in the fine print it says that **only the airfare TO Mexico was included in the price, not the airfare FROM Mexico.**

JUNIOR, HISTORY/PRE-LAW, OHIO STATE UNIVERSITY

I went to the Bahamas with Sunsplash tours on a scary chartered flight. We were left stranded in the Bahamas at a nasty, horrible, scary hotel that was crummy and we felt unsafe. We each paid $200 extra to stay at the Marriott instead.

GRADUATE, INTERNATIONAL STUDIES, FAIRFIELD UNIVERSITY

There was this five-day, four-night getaway to Cancun for $199. All you had to do was buy a plane ticket, put down a $1,000 security deposit, and buy or supply your own food. Well, the room was left in "unsatisfactory" condition, and **MY BUDDIES AND I LOST OUR DEPOSIT.**

SOPHOMORE, BIOLOGICAL SCIENCE, FLORIDA STATE UNIVERSITY

The Pitt Outdoors Club at my school took a trip to Key Largo and Key West and it was only $250 for the week. However, we camped on the beach during a tropical storm.

JUNIOR, PRE-PHYSICAL THERAPY/SPORTS MEDICINE, UNIVERSITY OF PITTSBURGH

The catch on, say, a $700 trip to Honduras for the week is that you have to volunteer to do heavy labor for poor kids and such for the entire week. I don't know if that's so much a "catch" as a Habitat for Humanity project, but the two seem interchangeable.

JUNIOR, HISTORY, DREW UNIVERSITY

If your budget is tight, any deal looks like a good one, but don't be fooled. Here's how to make sure you're getting a legitimate spring break offer:

Check for hidden fees. There are such things as port fees, which are the fees a cruise ship pays to dock at a port outside the United States, and customs taxes, which are fees you have to pay on items you buy in the country that you're taking back home with you. Read all the fine print and don't expect the person who's selling you the travel package to be up front about all the details.

Do your research. Deal with a travel agency or packager that someone you know has used before. Call the hotels and the airlines that have been booked for you, and make sure they have a working relationship with the company who is booking your spring break deal (so you don't get stranded at the airport or without a place to stay). You can also call the Better Business Bureau or look up a travel company on betterbusinessbureau.com to find out if there have been any complaints posted against them.

- **Know your destination.** Check for travel warnings and official U.S. government recommendations for travelers at whitehouse.gov/government/handbook/travel.html. This site has links to information about obtaining passports and visas, tips for travel safety, and listings of travel bureaus around the United States.

- **Always travel armed with several guidebooks.** That way you can cross-reference information on accommodations and transportation.

STUDENTS SAY: Don't Be Fooled By Attractive Packaging

Make sure you really investigate "all inclusive." Be sure your deal really includes everything from food to drinks to clubs as well.

JUNIOR, SOCIOLOGY, UNIVERSITY OF MINNESOTA

Always be wary of an ad in the back of a newspaper or on a flyer in a random classroom. I came across a deal for a trip to Cancun. Everything seemed pretty and packaged until I did the research.

SOPHOMORE, JOURNALISM, UNIVERSITY OF COLORADO—BOULDER

I knew people who were burned on spring break deals to Puerto Vallarta. It turned out that you couldn't fly from the United States because the planes weren't certified by the FAA, so they had to drive to Tijuana from UCLA. When they got there, there were chickens on the plane in the passenger compartment. It was just a bad scene. If it sounds too good to be true—it is.

SENIOR, ECONOMICS, UNIVERSITY OF CALIFORNIA—SANTA CRUZ

There are horror stories galore, but don't get scared away from taking a well-deserved break. You're thinking palm trees, a hammock, maybe a beachside hotel room . . . well, you might not be able to get the most luxurious package on your budget, but there are ways to ensure a great time on spring break:

◉ If you decide to leave stateside, or even just travel within the United States, check out your local travel agency for student rates on hotels and flight/hotel packages.

◉ Check out statravel.com and studentuniverse.com to find information on travel insurance, book flights, and to find out how to obtain an ISIC (international student identification card), which can get you a break on hotel and flight rates for a year.

When all else fails, be creative. The best spring breaks happen when you do what you want to do with who you want to do it. Take a road trip home for free meals and free rooms, or check out all the regional treasures you've never had time to visit before.

TRAVEL INSURANCE

WHY YOU NEED IT: Even though it's an added expense, it's important to protect your belongings, including your plane ticket, in case they are stolen or lost. Having insurance also guarantees that you'll get most or all of your money back if you have to cancel the trip.

WHERE YOU CAN GET IT: Check with your travel agent, your hotel, or your local travel bureau.

STUDENTS SAY: Get In The Know On Spring Break Deals

I grew up by a spring break hot spot, so I knew all about it. **Call hotels or rental agencies about six months to a year in advance**. If it is a package deal, try to find someone who has used/done that one before. It is easy to find people to recommend the best hotels, hot spots, and restaurants if they have been there before.

GRADUATE, INTERNATIONAL BUSINESS, UNIVERSITY OF TEXAS—AUSTIN

I worked for a company that sold spring break trips. The truth is that they are all about equal, and as long as you don't have fantasies of a luxurious resort vacation and are a realistic college kid just looking for a party with other realistic college kids, then you won't feel ripped off.

JUNIOR, PSYCHOLOGY, CLEMSON UNIVERSITY

Many students try to make money by promoting spring break packages on their campus. They receive a commission based on their package sales/registrations. I have always ignored these promotions. If a student wants to take a successful spring break trip, he needs to plan it well ahead of time, when airfare is lower, with a legitimate travel agency.

SENIOR, LEGAL STUDIES, UNIVERSITY OF CENTRAL FLORIDA

I hear about these deals to Cancun and ski resorts. I don't look twice at them, though. Usually, if you're smart, you can create your own spring break deal. That's how a lot of my friends do it. The people who offer the deals are usually a third party and tack their expense into the package. CUT OUT THE MIDDLEMAN AND DEAL DIRECTLY WITH THE HOTELS or find a place like priceline.com.

SOPHOMORE, ECONOMICS, UNIVERSITY OF TEXAS—AUSTIN

I saw a deal that included round-trip airfare plus hotel accommodations to Oahu for only $500. But this one was for real and I went with a friend and we had an amazing time!!

SENIOR, POLITICAL SCIENCE, UNIVERSITY OF OKLAHOMA

Spring break is for sleep. I am not one of those "Girls Gone Wild" types. Simply take it easy, go out with friends, and go to the beach if possible. You can gather funds from a few roommates and rent for the weekend.

GRADUATE, ENGLISH, FLORIDA INTERNATIONAL UNIVERSITY

If you're tight for money, **a relaxing spring break doing nothing is just as good.** After all, it *is* called a break.

SOPHOMORE, BIOLOGY/PRE-MEDICINE, MESA STATE COLLEGE

Acquaint yourself with the foreign students on campus. They may very well invite you to visit them in their home country during breaks, thereby cutting down on accommodation expenses. I have friends in France who stay with me for a week each August, and who put me up each year in the heart of Paris! We all win.

SENIOR, COMMUNICATION, SANTA BARBARA CITY COLLEGE

Now that you've found a legitimate, cheap option, the next step is to prepare to have a great time once you get to your spring break destination. Here's how to make sure your vacation is smooth sailing from the moment you step off the plane:

- Remember that all tourist destinations will be heavily attended by pickpocketers and other criminal professionals who will try to rip you off. Never give your bags to anyone or get in a car with a non-official taxi driver. You might wind up having to buy yourself a whole new wardrobe, or worse, go through the hassle of replacing your passport from abroad.

- If the sky looks threatening, don't despair. There are many ways to get around bad weather. Check out a museum, or if your hotel has a concierge, ask him about other interesting indoor activities.

- Keep important belongings in a hotel safe. Trust no one, not even the hotel staff.

- Avoid extra charges by checking out on time, keeping your room in good shape, and not making calls from your hotel phone (even local calls often come with an extra charge).

INSIDER TIP

Talk to locals—they'll know where the good, cheap non-touristy places are to eat and sightsee.

My friends talked me in to driving to Myrtle Beach, South Carolina, because they'd booked an awesome beachfront condo for cheap. We got there and it was a complete dump, not on the beach, and lizards were running rampant in the room. We spent our first day there trying to find another room but every place was booked. We finally got an "emergency" room booked in this oceanfront, nice condo! I told them it was just me and a friend staying there, so five of us had to share a king-size bed!

SENIOR, BIOLOGY, UNIVERSITY OF ARKANSAS

INSIDER TIP

Always carry xeroxed copies of your passport and travel documents in several places, including on you and in your suitcase.

I went on one "college trip" to San Felipe, Mexico, that was a little less than the pictures had promised in regards to the accommodations. At least one person per every three rooms had something stolen by the housekeepers.

JUNIOR, LITERATURE AND WRITING,
CALIFORNIA STATE UNIVERSITY — SAN MARCOS

"Each year, more than 2,500 American citizens are arrested abroad—about half on narcotics charges, including possession of very small amounts of illegal substances. A drug that may be legal in one country may not be legal in a neighboring nation. Some young people are victimized because they may be unaware of the laws, customs, or standards of the country they are visiting."

"Travel Safety Information for Students Fact Sheet." U.S. Department of State, Bureau of Consular Affairs, American Citizens Services. http://travel.state.gov/spring_break.html

Of course, you don't travel only for spring break. Travel costs in college can add up, especially when you get homesick. The next chapter details how you can save money on your other collegiate journeys.

WEB RESOURCES

www.aaa.com – Get information on travel discounts here, as well as online directions and links to order TripTiks, maps with specific routes based on individual traveling plans.

www.lonelyplanet.com – This site has extensive destination guides, information on healthy traveling, and message boards for travelers to exchange travel advice.

http://travel.state.gov/travel/livingabroad_springbreak.html – The U.S. government's tip sheet for student travelers. Includes links to updates of all the standing U.S. government travel warnings and consular information sheets (travel tips, warnings, details on safety) for every country in the world.

www.counciltravel.com – Offers student rates for flights and travel insurance.

www.travelguard.com – Online resource for travel insurance.

TRAVELING "BROKE" STYLE 13

Greyhound is cheap, but friends with cars are even cheaper!

JUNIOR, GENERAL MUSIC, UNIVERSITY OF OREGON

Whether you need some TLC from your mom or just want to relax and party with your friends, you're going to have to deal with the complications of traveling home many times throughout your college years. Whether you get there by bus, train, plane, or car, we'll tell you how to get there for less.

SIT BACK AND TAKE A RIDE: BUSES AND TRAINS

You live close by but don't have a car, or you're saving up for a camping trip with the outdoor club and you don't want to spluge on airfare—there are many reasons students opt to take buses or trains versus flying. Here's how to make your decision to ride the rails or bus work best for your budget.

- **Research bus or train options.** Both Amtrak and Greyhound have student deals and all of their travel info is available online.

- **Be flexible.** Try making a reservation for off-peak hours or for a day later than your classmates are traveling.

- **Investigate open tickets for trains or buses that run regularly all day.** This option might save you money since you don't have a guaranteed seat.

STUDENTS SAY: Trains and Buses Get You There Cheaply

Greyhound buses are really cheap and not so bad if you go to school less than five hours from home. Check the schedules and TAKE THE EXPRESS ROUTE WITH FEWER STOPS. Also buy the student advantage card and use it, or ask for student discounts.

SOPHOMORE, ECONOMICS/HISTORY, TUFTS UNIVERSITY

I bought a train pass that was worth 10 one-way trips, so it translated to less money per trip than the usual price.

JUNIOR, BIOLOGY, UNIVERSITY OF CALIFORNIA—DAVIS

For coast-to-coast travel or if you're looking to get home quickly, flying is the way to go. Of course, shorter traveling times and more convenience require more money from you. Check out these tips and fly for less:

- **Look for deals online.** Try websites like priceline.com and hotwire.com for low fares. The only drawback is that you won't know flight details (e.g., your seat number or flight times) until after you've purchased your tickets.

- **Consider traveling standby.** Give up your seat on an overbooked flight and you'll get bumped up to first class on your rescheduled flight or get offered a free flight. The hours are rough and nothing's guaranteed, but it's a cheaper deal and eventually, though it might be a day later than you wanted, you'll fly home at a cheaper price.

FINDING AIRFARES ON THE WEB

Unless you're traveling internationally or planning a vacation with a hotel stay, chances are you'll go to the Web to get your tickets home for winter break. There are many, many options now for buying tickets online. Here are some things to keep in mind:

- **Read the fine print.** Make sure the website you're using is clear about their return and scheduling policies.
- **Talk to people who've traveled to the same destination.** They can tell you the best way to go about getting airline tickets online (i.e., which site to use). If no one's ever heard of a certain website, chances are you're better off staying away.
- **Some online sites are directly associated with specific airlines.** Using a site like this will give you the peace of mind of receiving your information and confirmation numbers—directly from the airline.
- **Online tickets have different restrictions than paper tickets.** They also have different return and exchange policies than paper tickets. If you change your travel plans, you might have to pay a lot more to change your ticket or you might have to buy a new one altogether.

The best time to buy an online ticket is around 3 or 4 A.M. This is because the companies update their systems and lower the prices on tickets that aren't selling. Also, if you can wait, buy tickets that can be used in the next day or two; they are often very cheap.

JUNIOR, BIOLOGY, CARNEGIE MELLON UNIVERSITY

If you live pretty far away like me (I live across the country) and you have to fly, then I'd advise getting tickets two to three months ahead of time so you don't have to pay $500 just to go home.

JUNIOR, CRIMINAL JUSTICE, INDIANA UNIVERSITY—BLOOMINGTON

Definitely check into frequent flier programs and family plans (for sharing flier miles).

SENIOR, PSYCHOLOGY, TEXAS CHRISTIAN UNIVERSITY

If you are not in a huge hurry to get home or back to school, airlines always overbook flights, so **fly on a heavy travel day and offer your ticket to someone who is on standby when the attendants ask.** The airline will get you to your destination later that day or the next, but they give you a free round-trip flight to anywhere in the nation to be used within one year! These come in handy.

SENIOR, COMMUNICATION, CLEMSON UNIVERSITY

My home is near a very small airport, serviced only by one airline; consequently, flight prices are very high. So I would always fly into the big international airport about seven hours away and drive home with friends who lived there.

GRADUATE, PSYCHOLOGY, UNIVERSITY OF SOUTHERN CALIFORNIA — LOS ANGELES

Traveling Monday through Thursday can **save you money**—off peak days are generally less expensive.

GRADUATE, POLITICAL SCIENCE, UNIVERSITY OF CALIFORNIA—LOS ANGELES

There are often **student discounts on airline tickets** through most major credit cards so be sure to check with your credit card company before buying.

GRADUATE, EDUCATION, UNIVERSITY OF CALIFORNIA—BERKELEY

ON THE ROAD TIPS

There's nothing like a road trip to get yourself where you want to go with the thrill of the unexpected thrown in. But traveling by car can get expensive when you factor in gas prices, tolls, and stops along the highway for fast food. Here are some tips for saving money when traveling by car:

- Check your school's ride board. There's usually a place, either online or in the student center, where people offering rides and people needing rides are listed. Just remember that you might end up in a car with your ex–best friend's roommate's boyfriend. On the other hand, you'll save big time just by splitting gas costs.
- Once you hit the road, make sure you have a plan for what to do if you get a flat or have engine trouble. If you stop at a repair shop, agree on a price beforehand so you don't get ripped off.
- Consider getting an automobile club membership, which provides insurance and essential services like roadside assistance if you run out of gas or blow a tire.

Carpool. My first roommate and I graduated from the same high school so we drove home together a lot. The problem was he liked country music and outweighed me by about 100 pounds, so there was nothing I could do about changing the station.

GRADUATE, PSYCHOLOGY, WASHINGTON STATE UNIVERSITY

Bum rides from other people. Put up signs in the dorms if you're looking to go somewhere; you never know if someone who needs company is heading your way.

JUNIOR, MARKETING/GRAPHIC DESIGN, UNIVERSITY OF NOTRE DAME

If you have a car, let people know when you are driving somewhere . . . **someone else probably wants to go there and will pay you $20 to do what you are already doing.**

JUNIOR, GOVERNMENT/COMPUTER SCIENCE, WESLEYAN UNIVERSITY

If you carpool, PACK LUNCHES. It is better than stopping for food and spending unnecessary funds when you are almost home.

JUNIOR, CIVIL ENGINEERING, UNIVERSITY OF NEW MEXICO

Carpooling sucks because you could go home at weird hours and if your ride has car troubles, they are partly your troubles, too!

JUNIOR, LAW AND SOCIAL THOUGHT, UNIVERSITY OF TOLEDO

Get one of those E-ZPass things. Sometimes they have discounts.

JUNIOR, BIOCHEMISTRY, UNIVERSITY OF MARYLAND

Try to drive at or below the speed limit, if possible. GOING SLOWLY WILL SAVE YOU MONEY ON GAS.

SOPHOMORE, CHEMICAL ENGINEERING, UNIVERSITY OF KANSAS

Once I got my car, I made a point to find the cheapest gas stations in my town and on the way home. Very helpful. Also, keep your car in decent shape so it doesn't leak oil or guzzle gas, which will cost way more in the long run.

JUNIOR, BIOLOGY, UNIVERSITY OF CALIFORNIA—DAVIS

My home is a two-hour drive from college so my only expense is gas. **Let your parents borrow your car when it's on empty so they have to fill it.**

SOPHOMORE, HUMAN DEVELOPMENT AND FAMILY LIFE, UNIVERSITY OF KANSAS

Buy gas on Wednesday or Thursday morning. The cost goes up after that.

JUNIOR, ENGLISH LANGUAGE AND LITERATURE, UNIVERSITY OF MICHIGAN—ANN ARBOR

Buy gas at the coolest time of the day—the density is less.

SENIOR, BIOCHEMISTRY, UNIVERSITY OF ARKANSAS

You've finished with your travels, so now it's back to reality—and day-to-day living at college. The next chapter has tips for keeping down housing costs both off-campus and in the dorms.

WEB RESOURCES

For airline tickets:

www.expedia.com

www.onetravel.com

www.cheaptickets.com

www.counciltravel.com

For train tickets:

www.amtrak.com

For bus tickets:

www.greyhound.com

For car emergencies:

www.aaa.com

THE COST OF LIVING: HOUSING 14

There are a million and one bills you have to pay! No one ever told me I would have to pay to breathe my own air!

JUNIOR, BIOLOGY, TEMPLE UNIVERSITY

ROOMMATE RULES

What's worse than one broke college student trying to figure out how to make ends meet? Throwing in another broke college student and figuring out how to split the bills. There are several ways to approach paying bills in a roommate or multi-roommate living situation:

◉ Have one person pay the bill and have everyone pay him back each month. It's best to have everyone pay the person before he sends out the check for the total amount.

◉ Split the bills, with each roommate writing individual checks to each company. While it means writing more checks, each roommate will have to pay their individual portion to get the bill paid.

◉ Create a communal account to which everyone contributes an agreed upon amount and pay your bills with that money.

My roommate and I decided that we would share expenses for groceries. This started out as a good idea but because we never set guidelines for expenses, my half of the groceries was always way out of my budget. **Be sure to set guidelines.**

GRADUATE, SOCIOLOGY, MARQUETTE UNIVERSITY

It's hard to split a gas/electric/cable bill with housemates. You just need to elect one person to handle it and get people to write him a check, and make sure they pay promptly. Individual stuff gets too confusing.

JUNIOR, BIOLOGY, WASHINGTON AND LEE UNIVERSITY

When buying things for the apartment like Internet hubs, it's hard to split the cost because only one person will get to keep it in the end. But I don't think that person should pay for the whole thing either. A resolution would be that the person who gets to keep it pays a little more, but the others also pay some of the cost.

SOPHOMORE, INTEGRATIVE BIOLOGY, UNIVERSITY OF CALIFORNIA—BERKELEY

We had some trouble with the heating bill being so high. People in the house kept playing with the thermostat. Someone would put it higher and then someone else would lower it. Last month, we paid more than $200. That was a pain. We talked about it and agreed to set it at 68 degrees and no one's touched it, and we can't blame anyone for it.

JUNIOR, CRIMINAL JUSTICE, INDIANA UNIVERSITY—BLOOMINGTON

You have to remember to sit down with your roommates and pay bills twice a month or you will end up paying a boatload in late charges.

GRADUATE, SPEECH COMMUNICATIONS, KANSAS STATE UNIVERSITY

WHEN YOU END UP FOOTING THE BILL . . .

It's been so great living with a friend that when she doesn't pay you back for the phone bill for two months, you figure she's just short on cash. Then you remember—she never paid you back for her half of the electric bill from last month either. Come to think of it, did she ever pay you back for your Ramen that she's been taking for her nightly midnight snack? As careful as you are in planning your finances, there are always unknown factors that can throw off your precarious financial balance, the biggest one being other people.

Here are some ways to broach the subject if your roommate has been taking advantage of your generosity—let's call it excessive "borrowing."

Set a straightforward precedent. Make it clear that you're not going to let these discrepancies slide. If your roommate sees you paying her portion of the bills or you allow her to keep eating the food that you paid for, there's no reason for her to stop. Try to approach her rationally by saying something like, "I've noticed that you haven't been paying me back for groceries that you use. I'm going to keep a running list, and you need to pay me back before the end of each month."

⊚ **Let your roommate know you're broke, too.** You don't owe anyone any favors when it comes to money. Always look out for number one when you're trying to keep yourself out of the red: "I can't afford to pay your half of the phone bill and mine."

⊚ **Suggest alternative arrangements.** "If you'd like, I can pick you up the same snacks and you can pay me back." Or, "If you can't manage to pay your part of the phone bill, maybe we should use phone cards or cell phones instead."

My roommate would always go to the grocery store with us and never buy anything because she didn't have the money. She would say she didn't want to eat anything. Then when she was hungry, she would help herself to our food.

JUNIOR, MARKETING, QUINNIPIAC UNIVERSITY

MY ROOMMATES AND I USED TO FIGHT OVER EVERY SINGLE BILL WE HAD. They had to determine down to the penny what we owed. Phone bills were the worst. We had to sit and go through every phone call to figure out EXACTLY who owed what, including tax and extras like call waiting. Sharing groceries was a problem, too. Some people would get mad if they went to get something and there was none left. We avoided this by buying our own groceries and never using one another's things.

SENIOR, PSYCHOLOGY/ELEMENTARY EDUCATION,
INDIANA UNIVERSITY OF PENNSYLVANIA AND SAINT VINCENT COLLEGE

There is the issue of food, but I always had a laissez-faire, contribute-as-much-as-you-eat attitude, and we didn't have too many problems. This does become troublesome if you have a mooching roommate, but then if that's the case, you've probably got bigger problems.

JUNIOR, ENGLISH, UNIVERSITY OF PUGET SOUND AND SOUTHERN METHODIST UNIVERSITY

My freshman year, there was some tension with my roommate over how to split the phone costs because he wanted options (Caller ID, call waiting, etc.) that I felt we didn't need. So the lesson I learned was: **Learn how to compromise.** It is MUCH MORE WORTH THE MONEY to have a great year with your roommate than to have tension over a few bucks.

GRADUATE, MUSIC/HUMAN BIOLOGY, STANFORD UNIVERSITY

One year I lived with my boyfriend and his friend. I was the only one with a checking account, a credit card, and a driver's license. I paid the bills and collected cash. It didn't work too well and to this day I am still paying off the debt from those deadbeats. You learn the hard way.

GRADUATE, BIOLOGY, MOORHEAD STATE UNIVERSITY

WHEN TALKING DOESN'T DO THE TRICK

 Usually you'll be able to resolve any conflicts with your roommates by being honest and clear about what needs to be paid and when and what items can be shared. But every once in a while, a roommate comes along who won't change his financially devious habits. Here are some resources for dealing with a wayward roommate:

- **Look into the legal side of things.** It might seem extreme, but don't rule out written contracts or agreements stating rules for paying bills or buying groceries. Showing your roommate that you're serious about keeping things straight might just be the kick in the pants he needs to shape up.

- **Get out while you can.** If things are really bad, there's no reason to watch your savings dwindle as your roommate stores up on your broccoli.

- **Go to a dean or financial officer for advice.** If you live on-campus, talk to an RA. Sharing conflicts between roommates isn't anything new to college advisers, so you can benefit from their wisdom and experience.

There were issues with roommates where I would end up buying more supplies at times. **WE BASICALLY ASSIGNED WHO BOUGHT WHAT AND CAME OUT WITH A REASONABLE AGREEMENT.** We knew what we each needed to buy and it was never a problem. Communication is very important.

SENIOR, PSYCHOLOGY, NEW YORK UNIVERSITY

Make sure that if you do split a large purchase, you have a contract or written agreement so that there can be no argument about what will happen to the merchandise when school ends or someone leaves.

GRADUATE, BIOLOGY, NORTH PARK UNIVERSITY

The solution to roommate conflicts can more often than not be resolved through the use of a simple, written contract. The parties will be bound to the terms of the contract, and should a problem arise, **THE POSSIBILITY OF BEING SUMMONED TO SMALL CLAIMS COURT** may itself provoke the other party to comply with the terms of the contract.

SENIOR, LEGAL STUDIES, UNIVERSITY OF CENTRAL FLORIDA

Roommate issues won't be where your financial concerns end. Renting an apartment incurs myriad costs, which you should be aware of *before* you decide whether or not to move off-campus. Here are some cost-related questions to help you get the most for your money:

- "How much is monthly rent? How much is the security deposit? When will you get your deposit back?
- If you have roommates, do you each sign the lease? Are you each responsible for your own share of the rent, or will you be expected to cover costs if one of the roommates doesn't pay? Are there extra fees for additional roommates?
- What date is the first rent payment due? On what date is rent due after that?
- Is there a deposit for keys or pets?
- Which utilities are you responsible for?
- What kind of trash removal facilities are provided for the building?"

Hadad, Roxana. "Questions to Ask When Looking for an Apartment." 2003. www.fastweb.com

LEASES AND LANDLORDS

Two bedrooms, a working fridge, and, amazingly enough, a dishwasher—you've found the perfect apartment! Now you'll have to put down a security deposit, which usually amounts to one month's rent, and you'll have to produce proof of your credit history. Remember, landlords aren't running college dorms. To get past the ingrained images of loud partying and property damage that many landlords associate with college life, check out these strategies to make you a better potential renter:

- "Offer a larger deposit as a show of good faith.
- Try to get a cosigner with a good credit history (usually your parents). The cosigner is equally obligated for the rent payments and other charges.
- Private landlords often have less restrictive policies than large apartment complexes. Prepare a set of character references and provide them up front."

"Landlord-Tenant Fact Sheet for College Students." Springboard Non-Profit Consumer Credit Management. www.credit.org

STUDENTS SAY: Watch Out for Off-Campus Money-Suckers

I didn't know how hard it is to get a landlord to give back the security deposit. Keep really good records and make sure you document damage already in the apartment or the landlord will stick you with it.

SENIOR, PUBLIC RELATIONS, BRIGHAM YOUNG UNIVERSITY

Last year, we had to pay for the "Common Building Damages." This meant that everyone who lived in the building had to split the cost of things like cleanup after parties, missing doorbell ringers, damage to the siding of the building—things that we did not do. It was really annoying but legally, they could do that.

JUNIOR, JOURNALISM, SYRACUSE UNIVERSITY

Trash bags are pretty expensive.

JUNIOR, PHYSICS, STATE UNIVERSITY OF NEW YORK—BINGHAMTON

STUDENTS SAY: It's a Different World

Off-campus is another world, but it was nothing I didn't expect or wasn't ready for. I had roommates and **we were all in it together.** We worked and we studied and we lived the college life . . . very well.

GRADUATE, BIOLOGY, MOORHEAD STATE UNIVERSITY

You're almost at the end! And we've saved the best for last—the crème de la crème of quotes from college students on how to make fast cash. Read on to find out the easiest and most creative ways to fill your wallet in the least amount of time.

WEB RESOURCES

www.udregistry.com – A "credit bureau" for landlords and an information site for consumers.

www.college-student-life.com/liveoffcampus.htm – This article, "Living Off Campus—How to Save Money," offers advice on the little things that add up when you're living off-campus and how to keep these costs down.

www.youcandealwithit.com – This site has a "moving on and moving out" section with questions to ask yourself when you're looking for an apartment.

FAST CASH 15

Ask everyone you know for a dollar. If you're popular, you might end up with a lot of money.

SENIOR, POLITICAL SCIENCE, UNIVERSITY OF WEST FLORIDA—PENSACOLA

Even the most budget-conscious college student needs to make some fast cash every once in a while. This chapter is dedicated to the students who have come up with surefire ways for easy money—read on for the real deal on getting cash fast.

Sometimes you could count cars that went by an intersection for 50 bucks an hour. Don't ask me why people wanted to know this information.

GRADUATE, EXERCISE SCIENCE, COLLEGE OF NEW JERSEY

STUDENTS SAY: Do Whatever It Takes

I did everything from cutting people's hair to helping people type and edit their papers. I also had parties and charged entrance fees. If you are in shape like I was since I played soccer, train sorority girls who are looking to lose weight so they can wiggle into the bikini they wore last year and lose the "freshman 15" pounds.

GRADUATE, PSYCHOLOGY, WASHINGTON STATE UNIVERSITY

I was a card dealer for a company that hired out dealers for parties and weddings. The people weren't gambling for money but for raffle tickets. I got tips a lot, too, because I said I was a starving college student.

GRADUATE, BIOLOGY, UNIVERSITY OF CALIFORNIA—DAVIS

I made glass-beaded fan pulls and sold old clothes to a consignment shop.

SENIOR, PSYCHOLOGY, UNIVERSITY OF ALABAMA—TUSCALOOSA

I keep a change jar so that when I need unexpected cash, I can go cash it in at one of those coin machines.

JUNIOR, MARKETING/SPANISH, UNIVERSITY OF ARIZONA

Offer to help clean other friends' houses . . . it's funny how students hate to clean ANYTHING!

SENIOR, PSYCHOLOGY, UNIVERSITY OF CALIFORNIA—DAVIS

Car washes. They're the best way to go.

JUNIOR, BIOLOGY, COLLEGE OF WILLIAM & MARY

You need it, they got it. According to students, these are the most popular methods for making fast money:

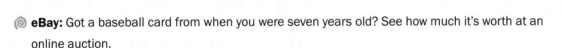

- **eBay:** Got a baseball card from when you were seven years old? See how much it's worth at an online auction.

- **Selling used books, clothes, furniture:** If you don't need it, put it up for sale—all it takes is word of mouth and a few signs advertising items for sale to the highest bidder. This is especially useful at the end of the year when you're moving and getting rid of stuff that you won't need in your living quarters the following year.

- **Baby-sitting:** It's the age-old option. Where there are children, there's baby-sitting.

I sign up for psychology experiments that pay per hour. I usually don't partake in anything that can be harmful.

JUNIOR, PSYCHOLOGY, UNIVERSITY OF CALIFORNIA—DAVIS

I got hired as a testing proctor for disability support services. I can study while I proctor the tests and get paid for doing virtually nothing.

JUNIOR, ART/PSYCHOLOGY, EAST CAROLINA UNIVERSITY

I used to tutor people who desperately needed help on difficult subjects such as chemistry and organic chemistry . . . and sometimes they'd be willing to pay $25 or $30 an hour. Great work!

JUNIOR, NUCLEAR MEDICINE/CHEMISTRY, UNIVERSITY OF THE INCARNATE WORD

Sometimes I sold my typing skills to guys who couldn't type.

GRADUATE, SOCIOLOGY, MARQUETTE UNIVERSITY

I sold T-shirts with catchy phrases on them for $10 each in-between classes.

SENIOR, ENGLISH, UNIVERSITY OF CALIFORNIA—SANTA CRUZ

STUDENTS SAY: More Fast Cash Strategies . . . At Your Own Risk

Rally around something that is happening on-campus, make shirts for it, and sell them for $10 apiece . . . sporting events and concerts work well.

JUNIOR, GOVERNMENT/COMPUTER SCIENCE, WESLEYAN UNIVERSITY

We threw a house party and charged everyone $5. WE MADE A LOAD OF MONEY. This should only be done, of course, when you don't have studying to do and when you can monitor who is coming to your house so that it doesn't get too rowdy!

JUNIOR, BIOLOGY, UNIVERSITY OF WISCONSIN — MILWAUKEE

I actually loaned out my car for the evenings (most people at UCLA don't have cars because they can't get parking permits). They paid me money and returned it with a full tank. Although it worked for me, it's slightly risky and quite illegal, so I wouldn't suggest it.

SOPHOMORE, BIOLOGY, UNIVERSITY OF CALIFORNIA — LOS ANGELES

I'm a bartender as well as an Avon representative. **Bartending brings fast cash,** and Avon brings in cash as long as I get in touch with a lot of people.

SENIOR, BIOLOGY, KEAN UNIVERSITY

Since I am mechanically inclined, I am able to fix people's cars and get paid for it.

JUNIOR, MOLECULAR CELL BIOLOGY, SAN DIEGO STATE UNIVERSITY

Quarters; they are hard to come by.

SENIOR, CHEMISTRY/MATH, DRURY UNIVERSITY

A digital camera—it's great to take pictures of everyone and you can download them on the computer so you don't have to spend megabucks developing film. I am sure the pictures taken on the camera will last forever.

SOPHOMORE, JOURNALISM, UNIVERSITY OF COLORADO—BOULDER

A tool box and jumper cables.

SENIOR, NURSING, UNIVERSITY OF KANSAS—LAWRENCE

The George Foreman grill—essential for any college student. Other than that, clothes.

GRADUATE, COMMUNICATION AND CULTURE, UNIVERSITY OF INDIANA—BLOOMINGTON

Gift certificates to local restaurants and bookstores.

SENIOR, POLITICAL SCIENCE/INTERNATIONAL STUDIES, NORTHWESTERN UNIVERSITY

A computer! Thanks Mom and Dad!

JUNIOR, MARKETING, ARIZONA STATE UNIVERSITY

A big box filled with supplies (printer ink, cleaning stuff, trash bags—all of the little things that add up quickly).

SENIOR, SPANISH/ANTHROPOLOGY, UNIVERSITY OF SOUTH DAKOTA—VERMILLION

CONCLUSION

Everyone has to face the reality of money being tight at one point or another. We hope we've shown you that if you watch every penny, make sure you know where your money's going, and know that it's well spent—even if you're an extremely broke student—you can have the time of your life in college.

Here are some pointers for how to keep your bank account healthy after graduation:

◉ **Pause and take stock of your finances.** Four years of partying, snacking, studying, road-tripping, and just plain living will take a good-sized chunk out of anyone's assets. You've done a good job keeping track of your financial well-being, but it's important to get a final read on your bank account before you take the next step. Remember that moving out can bring you both cost and gain: You have to pack up and ship your life to your next destination, but it's a great chance to get rid of that Chem 101 textbook and your ratty, old armchair for a few extra bucks for the road.

- **Consolidate your loans.** Once you're out of college, you're going to have to face those interest charges and repayment guidelines you were so careful to note when deciding how to pay your tuition. Make a plan fast, and the financial burden of college won't follow you far down your post-collegiate path.

- **Know where you stand.** Get a copy of your credit report on your way out of college. It's good to know your rating for future endeavors, like going to grad school (more loans!) or buying a new car or home.

And of course, we want to leave you with a few last words from the students themselves that are relevant both for college and as you make your way in the real world:

HAVE A GOOD ATTITUDE. Live frugally and you'll survive.

GRADUATE, POLITICAL SCIENCE, UNIVERSITY OF WISCONSIN—MADISON

Make your own cheap fun.

JUNIOR, BIOLOGY, HARDING UNIVERSITY

Save your change. While it may not seem like a lot, **pennies, nickels, and dimes add up when you're broke.**

GRADUATE, SOCIOLOGY, MARQUETTE UNIVERSITY